Collins

need to know?

Exotic
Pets

David Manning

Collins

First published in 2008 by
Collins, an imprint of
HarperCollins Publishers
77–85 Fulham Palace Road
Hammersmith, London W6 8JB

The Collins website address is:
www.collins.co.uk

Collins is a registered trademark of HarperCollins Publishers Limited
11 10 09 08
6 5 4 3 2 1

A catalogue record for this book is available from the British Library.

Created by: **SP Creative Design**
Editor: **Heather Thomas**
Designer: **Rolando Ugolini**
Series design: **Mark Thomson**

Photography
All images by Simon Murrell and David Manning, www.animalark.com.au
except for the following:
Jed Currey: Woma Python and Black Headed Python
Exo Terra vivariums Hagen
Can O' Food Zoo Med
Chris Mattison: American Green Toad

ISBN 978-0-0726275-5
Printed and bound by **Printing Express Ltd, Hong Kong**

Contents

Introduction 6

1   The vivarium **10**

2   Amphibians **40**

3   Reptiles: lizards and tortoises **70**

4   Reptiles: snakes **116**

5   Invertebrates **162**

Need to know more? 188

Index 190

Introduction

By picking up this book, you are probably either considering keeping exotic pets, or you already have an interest in them. Not only are many of these creatures extremely beautiful to look at but they are also much simpler to look after than some of the more traditional pet mammals and birds with whom we choose to share our lives.

Among the most popular pet amphibians, tree frogs are remarkably easy to look after and many species are suitable for handling by keepers.

Which species?

Whilst many species of exotic pets are easy to care for, there are some obvious considerations to bear in mind before purchasing one of these pets. In the case of children, for example, a parent or another adult must ultimately be responsible for the welfare of the chosen species. As a responsible herpetologist, in this book I have concentrated on species that meet the following criteria.

They are suitable for the novice keeper

I have tried to promote the care of the most easy-to-keep and interesting species, which are not too demanding in terms of time or space. At the same time, however, I have also included some of the most sought-after animals, such as chameleons and iguanas.

They are available from pet stores or breeders

All the species featured in the book are widely available from specialist breeders or pet stores and, wherever possible, from captive-bred stock. This will ensure that they are free from internal and external parasites and are most likely to adapt successfully to new homes.

Ease of care

I have listed the species that are featured within each section of this book in an 'ease-of-care' order. The easiest to keep appear first, graduating to those species that are more demanding in terms of equipment, space, owner's time and maintenance.

Conservation

Loss of natural habitat for housing or agricultural development, along with pollution and other negative human actions, is having a colossal impact on the rapidly decreasing numbers of reptiles, amphibians and invertebrates globally. An estimated 1,856 species of amphibians, i.e. 32 per cent of known species, are

Many snakes, like this Royal Python, are easy to keep and breed as pets.

Opposite: The endearing Leopard Gecko is a small lizard, very easy to tame and may be kept in small groups together in the vivarium.

'globally threatened' according to IUCN (International Union for the Conservation of Nature).

Captive breeding

Captive breeding offers an opportunity for the continued survival of many creatures. It is hoped that one day these may be reintroduced into the wild if their habitats can be saved. Captive breeding also helps reduce pressure on wild populations, teaches us about their life cycle and husbandry and provides us with healthier livestock. It is remarkably satisfying when you watch a snake hatch from an egg, or a batch of tadpoles metamorphose into their adult form.

These Australian Green Tree Frogs are a popular choice of pet and are widely available from captive bred stocks in Europe, the United States and Australia.

Responsible ownership and husbandry

The collection of certain animals from the wild and their trade between countries may, rightly or wrongly, be illegal. However, it is important that wherever you happen to live, you adhere to both your local and national rules and regulations. Responsible pet ownership and husbandry are always the right way to proceed.

A rewarding pastime

This book will help you not only to select a pet that suits you and your circumstances but also to learn more about these fascinating exotic animals and the whole subject of herptoculture, which can become a vastly rewarding and absorbing pastime for many keepers. A comprehensive range of the most popular species available are examined, with enough detail for even a novice keeper to successfully care for these intriguing creatures.

1 The vivarium

People have been keeping more unusual pets for centuries, and many make for surprisingly interesting and easy-to-keep companions. With patience and careful husbandry, it is possible, if desired, for the pet keeper to both enjoy and breed some of these wonderful creatures. In the home, a vivarium can be a beautiful and enchanting miniature habitat, which you and your pet can enjoy.

Choosing your pet

Before purchase, check with your local pet store, reptile club or wildlife agency to see if any restrictions apply with regard to keeping reptiles, amphibians or invertebrates as pets in the area where you live. At the time of writing, all the creatures in this book may be kept in the UK without any legal restrictions.

must know

Ask the person who is supplying the animal lots of questions. If they are reputable, they will expect you to ask them questions and should be able to assist you in selecting a suitable individual.

First steps

Read up all about the animals and their care and then decide on a species that will suit you and your circumstances best. Consider the accommodation, equipment, feeding and handling requirements.

Don't rush

Taking time is important – just like setting up an aquarium for fish, you need to check that a vivarium is running smoothly and the equipment functioning correctly before buying your pet. Monitor the temperature gradient and the humidity to ensure you have created the right environment.

With an aquarium or semi-aquatic set up, it is essential that you allow the water to age/mature, ideally for seven to ten days, so that the system functions to optimum effect.

Selection

Now that the vivarium is set up properly, you are ready to select your pet. To increase the chances of keeping your pet healthy and in tip-top condition you will need to choose a healthy individual, preferably a juvenile that has been captive bred by an established breeder.

Always look for specimens that:
- Are bright-eyed and alert looking
- Are good feeders
- Do not bolt, flee or cower.

Avoid specimens that:
- Have a dirty vent (the external opening of the urinary and genital systems) – caked-on faecal matter is a sure sign of illness
- Cannot support their weight or walk in an uncomfortable manner
- Have crooked limbs and lumps that are not a feature of that species
- Have little fat reserves on the tail
- Are the runt of a litter/batch.

Rearing containers

It is likely that many of the baby animals you are going to purchase will have been reared in what at first may seem like very unsuitable conditions – plastic boxes, 25 x 10 x 15cm (10 x 4 x 6in) with tiny air holes drilled into the lid for ventilation. Each box, containing a baby snake, for example, will be lined with paper and equipped with a tiny shelter and water dish. Providing it is warmed with a heater pad or cable, this is the ideal rearing container in which to nurture a young snake and raise it as a tame pet. To suddenly put such a fragile animal into your new larger vivarium can cause it great shock. It may feel vulnerable and refuse to feed or it may hide, never to be seen again. It is best to leave the young snake in its rearing container and when you feel the time is right – once it has grown a bit and feeds regularly – transfer it into its larger permanent set up.

Take time to select a healthy individual animal. This Spadefoot Toad is in excellent condition. It looks well fed and is alert and bright-eyed.

must know

Do not handle animals
after they have eaten or
when they are about to
moult or slough. If you
are transporting a pet,
it must be comfortable
and at a temperature
and humidity level that
will not cause suffering.

Where to obtain stock

Joining a reptile club or herpetological society is an
excellent way to obtain stock, find breeders and get
up-to-date information on suitable species. Ask
your family or friends; you will be surprised how
someone always seems to know someone who has
an interest in these pets. The internet is a good
source for information with thousands of websites
devoted to reptiles, amphibians and invertebrates.
The various reptile magazines published in most
countries are full of adverts, and your local library
will have other books on the subject. Even if your
local pet store does not stock reptiles, they will
probably know where to start looking.

Scientific or Latin names

People can easily get confused if only the common
names are used to discuss particular species: in the
UK the small African Python is called the Royal Python,
while in America it is known as the Ball Python. To

**Regular handling will enable both
you and your pet to get to know
each other better.**

avoid any confusion, zoologists use Latin names to describe all animals and plants. Karl von Linne, or Linnaeus as he is normally referred to, developed this two-name or binomial system in the 1700s. It is a useful tool, helping us classify and understand the natural world with a universally recognized system. So from China to the United States, the small African Python is known as *Python regius* and no one can mistake it for any other snake.

The Latin name is written in italics and usually follows the common name. In scientific journals, the common names are usually not used. When purchasing a pet, learn the Latin name and use it to avoid any confusion when doing further research.

Children, as well as adults, enjoy regular interaction with tame and friendly species of reptile.

Handling pets

Many of the species featured in this book are among the most handleable of all herptiles, and people can get great pleasure from this close contact with nature. However, some species are enjoyed aesthetically and once in the vivarium they are handled only when they are removed for cleaning to take place.

When handling your pet, check the environment is safe, e.g. do you need to close a door or window to prevent it from escaping if it takes flight or tries to hop away. Minimize the danger of a fall by sitting at a table or on the floor. Your pet is not a toy and handling by children must always be closely supervised by an adult.

Juvenile animals should only be handled occasionally and for short periods until they become tame or conditioned enough to sit still. Feeding your pet after a handling session is a good way to condition it to accepting human contact as a positive stimulus.

Adult supervision is always highly recommended when children handle small and delicate pets.

Amphibians

The mucus-covered skin of many amphibians protects them from bacterial infections and makes them difficult to handle. It is best to handle them with wet hands. Some amphibians have toxins in their skin, so do take care if you have any open wounds, as handling them may allow toxins to enter your body. Do not be put off handling them; during educational talks, my own tree frogs have been handled by many people several days a week for several years with no ill effect to man or frog. Most amphibians can be held in cupped hands or scooped up into small containers for transportation. These can be filled with a damp sponge to provide moisture. However, you must transport totally aquatic species in water.

Lizards

The dry skin and docility of the lizards that are featured in this book make them ideal candidates for more intimate contact – they are amongst the most handleable species. However, lizards should never be lifted by the tail – their ability to 'drop' them is well known.

Supported by caring hands, this gecko is learning to tolerate being handled by its keeper.

Snakes

Small snakes are easily supported in the hand – most will wrap around your fingers or wrist to feel comfortable. Never dangle them from the neck or tail, but support them along the length of their body. Heavier species should be held firmly and their weight supported. The novice keeper should not handle untamed snakes, as they need proper restraining. Transport your snakes in cloth bags or tied pillowcases. Smaller species or juveniles may be transported in their plastic rearing boxes.

Invertebrates

Many invertebrates are delicate and need careful handling. Do not disturb them if they are moulting. Caution is advised at all times when handling these creatures because most species have tiny hook-like claws that can easily get tangled up with clothing or may even snag a small child's skin. If in doubt, do not handle them.

must know

The benefits of keeping a vivarium pet can be summarized as follows:
1 You are unlikely to be allergic to an animal that has no fur or feathers.
2 Reptiles, amphibians and invertebrates may be kept in locations that prohibit the care of other species, e.g. a flat with no garden.
3 They are generally silent and do not require regular walks, annual veterinary inoculations or grooming.
4 Most species are easily maintained, requiring at most only a 10-minute daily feed and a cleaning regime that takes an hour or so each week.
5 Most species are content to live in a vivarium. Some, such as Milk Snakes, prefer small, secure accommodation – larger units may cause them stress.
6 Although a relationship may be established, vivarium pets, unlike dogs, will not be emotionally dependent on you. They will not feel lonely if you are out of the house during the day and many can be left safely for a weekend.
7 These fascinating creatures can help nurture an interest in natural history, conservation and, hopefully, a respect for all living things.

Housing your pet

To create the right environment for your pet, you must have an understanding of the types of accommodation and equipment that are available. Making the right choice is essential and should ensure that your pet enjoys a long and healthy life.

must know

must know

Always buy the best quality accommodation and equipment you can afford. Don't try to save money on what may be the most important aspect of your pet's welfare. The housing and equipment can cost more than the pet itself, but it will last and also provide an environment which is beneficial to the long-term wellbeing and health of your pet.

The vivarium

A vivarium or aquarium can be a beautiful and enchanting miniature habitat, which both you and your pet can enjoy. Many purpose-built vivaria are available, making it easy for you to select a secure unit and create the ideal conditions for the animals in your care. I generally encourage larger vivaria for most pets – they allow you to keep more individuals together and even to establish a community set up. The range of suitable vivaria can be divided into three main categories, as detailed below.

Glass

Glass is the most versatile option for housing. You can keep any animal mentioned in this book in a glass vivarium or aquarium. The latest Exo Terra vivariums (as pictured) are excellent and have a simple lock mechanism fitted to prevent any escapes; they are also well ventilated. I currently keep snakes, lizards, frogs and praying mantids in different-sized ones. Their disadvantage is they can't be stacked one on top of the other once your collection expands. Glass is easy to clean, hygienic and gives all-round visibility. It is important, however, to provide adequate cover and hiding places, so that your pet does not feel exposed.

Wood

Wooden or chipboard vivaria can be bought ready made or as flat packs for assembly at home. Their drawback is that they are less suitable for species requiring higher humidity levels as the moisture eventually seeps into and warps the wood. They are well insulated to keep herps warm with minimum loss of heat. They are functional and stackable but the least aesthetically pleasing of all the options.

Plastic

Several companies produce 'pet home' containers, which are stocked by most pet stores. They are useful for rearing juvenile snakes and lizards or for keeping and breeding invertebrates and live foods. They are colourful and quite cheap, but few are secure or large enough for long-term maintenance of larger snakes and lizards. Unless you can use only a heat pad, few have the potential to fit a spotlight or thermostat. They are especially useful if keeping animals in a room that is already heated. The acrylic material does deteriorate with age and is never as clear as glass, but, on the plus side, they are easy to move around and intrinsically safer than glass.

Lighting and heating

In a vivarium, try to offer the correct conditions for your pet to thrive in by providing suitable artificial heat and light. Spotlights are very useful for general lighting and provide hot basking spots, which are essential for thermoregulation. When 'night' falls after 12–16 hours of 'daytime', the temperature of a vivarium may drop quite significantly without the additional aid of a heater pad.

This glass vivarium is specifically designed for the care of many featured species.

Which lighting is best?

Nocturnal animals are most active in low-light conditions. Crepuscular species, such as toads and geckos, are most active at dawn and dusk when the light is reduced. Other species, such as the Bearded Dragon and Veiled Chameleon, will sunbathe in brilliant daylight at temperatures of up to 38°C (100°F) but they will still need a night-time dark period for sleep. The number of daylight hours and length of a season can also be important if you want to breed your pets. Bear all these factors in mind when lighting the vivarium.

must know

Herptiles and thermoregulation

A temperature gradient is essential for the successful maintenance of most herptiles. They thermoregulate, or move between different temperature zones, to warm up or cool down as required. Without adequate warmth, they cannot feed, digest food or even move about. At different times of the day or night, they will seek out an environment that suits their needs, and you must provide these different environmental conditions within the vivarium. A good temperature gradient can be established using a thermostat to control temperature. The chart below shows the effect of temperature on most herptiles. Most prefer a vivarium with temperature zones within the generally preferred range. Keep your animals at their preferred temperature; if it gets too hot or cold, they may suffer or even perish.

	Critically cold			Generally preferred range		Critically hot	
°C	0	4	10	20	35	45	50
°F	32	37	50	68	95	113	122

Full spectrum lighting

Most snakes, invertebrates and amphibians can, with a good diet and vitamin and mineral supplementation, thrive in captivity once the correct temperature gradient is provided with little need for what are called full spectrum lights. However, many day-active creatures need unfiltered sunlight to grow and develop healthy bones and skeletons. This can be provided artificially by buying full spectrum lighting, i.e. tubes and lamps designed to supply the ultraviolet, or UVA and UVB, like real sunlight. In essence, a full spectrum light is at the very least beneficial and often essential for herptiles that need to bask as well as many diurnal species.

A good selection of light tubes and bulbs are now available, including the self-ballasted Mercury Vapor lamps. It appears that herbivores and omnivores are most at risk of MBD (Metabolic Bone Disease), a condition that develops in some herptiles given inadequate exposure to real or artificial sunlight. Whenever possible, exposure to real sunlight is of huge benefit to all captive reptiles and amphibians.

Equipment

Your choice of pet will dictate what equipment you require to create the right environment. Every animal in this book may be housed successfully using a selection of the equipment described below.

Thermometer

One or more thermometers should be placed strategically near the main heat source and midway towards the cooler end of the vivarium in order to make accurate temperature checks.

Thermometer

Hygrometer

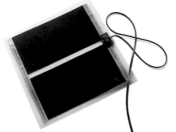

Heater pad

Ceramic heater

Thermostat

Hygrometer

This measures humidity and is a useful addition to any environment that needs regular monitoring.

Heater pads

A good range of low-, medium- and high-wattage pads are available. Low-wattage pads are ideal for heating invertebrates, or you may use higher wattage pads in conjunction with a thermostat. Never cover more than half the ground area in the vivarium with a heater pad.

Ceramic heaters

These powerful heaters are excellent for creating hotter basking areas for Bearded Dragons and Veiled Chameleons, although they don't provide any light. They must be thermostatically controlled, and pets and keepers must be protected from contact.

Thermostats

These are essential items for the regulation of temperature output of heaters in the vivarium.

Full spectrum tubes and bulbs

A range of products are available to suit the needs of most species. The tubes can provide essential UVA and UVB light and help promote plant health.

Spotlights and light bulbs

These are useful for heating and lighting, but they have no ultraviolet light content. Vivarium animals and furnishing should be protected from contact with them. For proper heat control, they are best regulated with a thermostat.

Water bowls

Keep these level with, or lower than, the surrounding ground level. You can use almost any suitably-sized dish or jam-jar lid. The manufactured type look more natural and have rough edges to give reptiles a better grip for getting in and out of the water. Keep the bowls clean and replenished with fresh water. Remember that some species prefer large bowls for bathing and others only drink from water droplets.

Hide

Hide rocks and wood

These give many herptiles and invertebrates a sense of security, i.e. a rock to crawl under. It is better to have too many than too few. Terrestrial animals want ground hides, whereas arboreal species prefer higher hides attached to the side of the vivarium. Cork bark is attractive and available in logs that are simple to break into small pieces. Avoid stacking heavy rocks: they may collapse and crush a pet that is digging.

Plastic plant

External and internal power filters

For optimum reptile and amphibian health, water purity is essential. The larger external power filters heat the water and keep it clean and flowing. I can't overstate how important water quality is, especially for semi or totally aquatic creatures.

Naturalistic backgrounds

Long pictures of natural landscapes are effective for any set up and come in many designs. They can be cut to the required length and simply affixed to the outside of a glass vivarium or inside a wooden one. If used inside, take care when attaching one as sticking tape can easily tear a reptile's skin.

Naturalistic background

Depending on the species you choose many options are available to create the right environment for your pet.

must know

It goes without saying
that you should read
instructions carefully
on all equipment and
follow normal electrical
safety rules. If in doubt,
you should contact a
qualified electrician.

Plastic and silk plants

Available in many colours and leaf forms, artificial
plants can provide cover, resting and climbing areas,
and make a set up look more attractive. They can be
washed and disinfected easily. A small pile of plastic
plants sprayed with water creates a humid micro-
climate appreciated even by desert species, especially
when sloughing, and helps stop dehydration. Never
site plastic plants and other furnishings too near to
any spotlights, light bulbs and other heaters.
Caution: some herbivorous reptiles will try to eat
them and may get sick.

Real plants

These are good for larger vivaria, especially those
with full spectrum lighting that help plants to thrive.
Sturdy plants, such as Philodendron (*Pothos*), are
ideal for Chameleons, whereas a spider plant suits

**Having created the right
environment, this Blue
Tongued Skink will thrive
in a vivarium.**

These artificial shelters provide a safe and secure retreat, which is essential for the well being of most pet herptiles.

Anolis or other lightweight species. There is no need to plant out a nicely arranged set up for larger, more boisterous species, such as the Blue-tongued Skink or Iguana, as they will destroy or flatten your efforts.

Substrates

Many substrates are available, and your choice will depend on the needs of your pet and your

1 The vivarium

must know

Books are a great source of information – visit your library or local book shop to see what is on offer. Many animal societies produce specialist publications and scientific papers giving more in-depth information on a particular species.

A variety of natural and artificial material may be used to create a visually appealing vivarium pet.

aesthetic preference. For ease of maintenance, many breeders and herpetologists keep lizards and snakes in bare, laboratory-style set ups with newspaper as a base. This may not affect the happiness of the animal at all, but I prefer naturalistic displays incorporating a mixture of substrates and furnishings. Listed below are some popular options, but if the substrate is clean and free from pests, parasites or toxins, many natural items found in your locality – twigs, leaves, stones and gravel – can all be safely utilized.

Play sand and pebbles

These are useful for desert species, and a mixture of sand, pebbles and woodchips will enhance the design

of most vivaria. Some specialist reptile stores sell decorative coloured sands for desert-style setups.

Wood or bark chips

A wide variety is available, but avoid the finest types because the particles may be taken in with food, causing digestive problems. This is a very common problem with captive lizards, especially juveniles.

Shredded aspen

This is a good choice, as it allows species to burrow into it for security, making it ideal for many snakes.

Leaf litter

Attractive seasonal leaves, conkers, pine cones, etc., can all enhance the appearance of a vivarium. These are best frozen to kill any resident pests.

Moss   **Wood chips**

Reptile grass

This is a green matting that is easily washed and very versatile. It can be placed on the ground, or on the side of the vivarium, for arboreal species.

Cork bark

Paper

Paper is easy to clean and replace but not very pleasing to the eye. Ensure that your vivarium pet is not under-stimulated by a bare or barren vivarium.

Pebbles

Leaves

Vermiculite

This natural product is excellent when wetted (and any excess moisture squeezed out) for providing an incubating medium for most eggs. It can be used as a substrate for spiders and other vivarium creatures.

As well as artificial options, many natural products are suitable as substrate and decoration.

Feeding your pet

All creatures need food to grow and thrive. Whereas herbivores eat only plant foods, some animals are less specific and eat other animals, insects, plants and fruits and are known as omnivores. Animals that feed only on insects are insectivores while those that feed on other animals are classed as carnivores.

A wide variety of both fruit and vegetables will be consumed by many of the featured species.

Successful feeding

You will need to determine which group your pet belongs to and offer it the right selection of foods, in sufficient quantity and quality, to satisfy its needs. Whatever the diet, it should supply that species' requirements in terms of fats, proteins, carbohydrates, vitamins and minerals. You also need to consider that feeding can be an important behavioural stimulus. Many insect-eating herptiles, for example, spend much of their life hunting for and catching food. Getting the feeding right for each animal is all part of successful pet management.

Herbivores

Many birds, mammals and invertebrates are herbivores, as are most tortoises and some lizards. However, many species supplement their diets with protein when available. Some is unintentionally consumed with plant matter; some intentionally sought.

A wide variety of fruit and vegetables can be shop bought, or grown in a pesticide-free garden or allotment. Amongst the most suitable are lettuce, broccoli, tomato, pear, apple, seasonal berries, e.g. raspberries and blackberries, dandelion flowers and their leaves and roots, spinach, carrot, cooked potato, cabbage, grasses and non-poisonous tree leaves, flowers and seeds.

Many complete foods are also available, as are balanced meals with added vitamins and minerals. Personally, I believe that you can do no better than provide your pet with a range of fresh foodstuffs, but complete foods are handy and not subject to seasonal availability. They are particularly useful if someone is caring for your pet in your absence.

Omnivores

Creatures that feed on plants and other animal species are omnivores – this category includes humans. Omnivores featured in this book, such as the Veiled Chameleon, Bearded Dragon and Blue-tongued Skink, will be satisfied with a combination of foods from the herbivore, insectivore and carnivore sections.

Individual preferences vary but Blue-tongued Skinks, for example, are usually partial to snails in their shells; an adult specimen will probably enjoy two or three snails and a quarter of a banana at one sitting. Insects are full of protein and few lizards will pass up the opportunity to eat these nutritious titbits – even those species considered herbivorous.

This Green Anole enjoys both hunting for and consuming its insect prey.

Insectivores

Due to increased interest in keeping and breeding herptiles, the range, quality and availability of live foods has grown greatly over the last few years. If you cannot obtain foodstuffs from your local pet store, you may easily purchase them by mail order. Insectivores, and most omnivores, will enjoy a selection from the following live foods, which are listed in order of size.

Locusts (*Locusta migratoria, Schistocerca gregaris*)
The fat-bodied, winged adults are ideal for large insectivores, although the spiky legs are not always appreciated. The young are referred to as hoppers. Usually measuring between 1–4cm (¹/₂–1¹/₂in), they are ideal for smaller lizards and frogs. Locusts tend to climb upwards, so are ideal for arboreal species.

Crickets (*Gryllus sp.*)
Probably the most widely available and inexpensive of all insect foods, these range from pinhead-sized hatchlings to adults over 3cm (1in) long. Various species are reared, but I prefer the black, silent crickets. They are plumper, quieter and less likely than the brown-coloured house cricket (*Acheta domestica*) to take up residence in the house if they escape. The hatchlings are excellent for the tiniest frog or newly-hatched lizard.

Mealworms (*Tenebrio sp and Zophobas sp.*)
Many species find these beetle larvae difficult to digest. Never use them exclusively, but only as part of a varied diet. Once they metamorphose into beetles, most reptiles will refuse to eat them.

These are the most popular live foods available to cater for the needs of your pet.

Waxworms *(Galleria sp.)*

The larvae of a small moth, these are also edible in adult form. Among the most nutritious and easily digested of live foods, they are useful for building up a weak, ill or stressed pet. Although excellent to use when taming lizards and frogs, don't feed them too often as they are very rich. They are fast movers and will wriggle into tiny nooks and crannies within the vivarium – feeding by hand will prohibit this.

Fruit flies *(Drosophila sp.)*

These little flies suit many baby lizards, frogs and invertebrates, such as praying mantids. They can be raised on fruit or special culture mixes. Since fruit flies quickly infest a location, you may prefer to order large flightless ones *(Trinidadian sp.)*.

A selection of pre-prepared canned foods is available at most good pet stores.

Other foods

The following foods are suitable for insectivores and omnivores. Some can be collected in the wild, whereas others are aquatic or carnivorous.

Collecting your own

Farmed live foods should be raised in hygienic conditions. One of the problems of collecting your own is that you always run the risk of introducing some parasite or unwanted guest. Having said this, one of the benefits of using wild-caught live foods is that they are packed with naturally acquired vitamins and minerals. They include the following:

• **Snails**: These calcium-rich creatures are liked by Blue-tongued Skinks, many toads and small lizards.
• **Worms**: Use earthworms purchased at a reptile shop or bred at home from bought varieties. Some

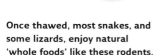

Once thawed, most snakes, and some lizards, enjoy natural 'whole foods' like these rodents.

species are toxic to amphibians and reptiles, especially those inhabiting compost heaps or rotting vegetation.
• **Spiders**: All spiders have fangs, but most are not dangerous to humans; adult supervision is advised. Check the species before collecting.

Aquatic foods
Foods for aquatic amphibians and rearing foods for animals at larval stages of development can be purchased from good pet stores. They include:
• **Tubifex**: These red aquatic worms are ideal for newts, Axolotls and many animals at the larval/tadpole stages.
• **Daphnia**: These crustaceans are found in ponds.
• **Brine shrimp** (*Artemia sp*): These may be bought alive or as eggs and require a salty solution that should be filtered before being offered as food.
• **Freshwater shrimp**: These are ideal for Axolotls, newts and Oriental Fire-bellied Toads.
• **Pond pellets and flaked fish foods**: Some Axolotls and aquatic frogs and newts will readily accept pellets. Most tadpoles will munch on flaked fish food, a complete and nutritious foodstuff.

Carnivores
The term 'carnivore' is largely used to describe flesh-eating animals. Within this book, the only true carnivores are snakes. For most of their lives, snakes in captivity will accept dead, thawed-out rodents, and are known as 'defrost feeders'. The rodents may be purchased ready frozen. For humane reasons, your pets should not be fed live vertebrate food. Snakes consume their food whole, so there is no mess or leftovers, and it would seem that their

vitamin and mineral requirements are met by their small rodent diet. Supplements are not generally needed, although you may add vitamin drops to the snake's water occasionally. Rodents fed include:

• **Mice** (*Mus musculus*): These are the best and most popular foodstuff for snakes. Juvenile, hairless mice, called pinkies, are an ideal size for hatchlings and juvenile snakes. Fuzzies, juvenile haired mice, are the next size up. Purchase them ready-frozen from your pet store or specialist herpetological supplier.

• **Rats** (*Rattus*): Small and medium-sized rats, preferably brown or black in colour, are a good-sized food for Royals and larger Kingsnakes.

• **Other rodents** Many smaller rodents are accepted by a variety of snakes – gerbils are particularly favoured by Royals. All frozen rodents should be fed to your pet only once they are thawed and warmed. Should you breed your own, rodents must be kept and then killed in a humane way.

Feeding snakes

Some processed snake foods are now available, but they are more expensive than rodents and I don't think they are necessary. Many species prefer to feed at dawn or dusk, or at least in low-light conditions. Offer your pet a thawed-out rodent held by its tail, using long tweezers. It should be accepted readily if a snake is hungry and not nervous. For many snakes, especially juveniles, leave the food in a hide box overnight, where the snake can find it at its leisure and then consume it in peace. Uneaten food should be removed and disposed of – do not re-freeze it.

Conveniently for the pet keeper, snakes consume their food whole and there is no mess.

Sometimes a bit of variety in the diet helps. This Axolotl enjoys the occasional earthworm.

Supplements

A range of products are now available for herptiles. The most important ones for many species contain added vitamins and minerals. Some new products claim to provide the UVA and UVB requirements of basking species in a liquid form. Use all products in moderation and at the recommended dose.

Feeding tips

Some people prefer to feed their pet in a separate container to the one in which it lives. Plastic pet homes are ideal and can also be used to keep your live foods. With this method, it may be easier to monitor how much is eaten by each pet. It may also train your pet to accept being handled first before receiving its food reward in its feeding box. It is important to keep and breed your live foods in hygienic and humane conditions. Care instructions should be available from your supplier or pet centre.

When pets refuse to feed

Species can stop feeding for many reasons. If you have had your pet for a while, it is likely that it is well fed, with built up fat reserves, and is 'full'. After a short break (a few days for a lizard to several months for a snake) it will continue to feed normally, so do not worry if it refuses food occasionally. However, there are times when you should be concerned about lack of appetite, such as:

• If you have just acquired it, and it has not eaten at all within the first week or so.

• It is getting thin or weak, or becoming less active.

If your pet is not eating, then check the following:

• Have you created the right environment? Is the unit warm enough or too warm? Is there enough water?

• Have you offered foods of the right type and size? Is the live food hassling your pet? Is the food offered in the right place and at the right time of day?

• Is your pet sloughing? Most species will refuse foods at this time but are hungry again afterwards.

Praying Mantids enjoy hunting live insect prey and prefer insects that will climb up onto twigs and branches in their vivarium.

Health and preventative care

Most health problems can be prevented, since the major cause of herptile ill health is poor husbandry or injury caused by you or another animal. By providing the correct environment, which is hygienically maintained, with the right quantity and quality of foods, most health problems can be prevented easily.

must know

Vitamin and mineral supplements are essential for many species. Give the correct dosage, as a lack, or excess, of vitamins and minerals can lead to health problems. They are very important for juveniles which are developing quickly. Always be sure to follow the manufacturers' guidelines.

Buying healthy specimens

I recommend that novices purchase captive-bred specimens wherever possible. Imported, wild-caught species are more likely to suffer from internal and external parasites and bacterial infections. Many of these problems can be overcome with correct medication and laboratory-style/quarantine housing. Contact your specialist society or dealer for advice if you think your pet has problems of this nature. If you think your pet is sick or suffering, contact a herptile proficient veterinarian immediately.

Obesity

Obesity is a major health risk for all pets. Too much food or a diet too high in preferred or fatty foods can cause serious problems. It is impossible to state exactly what quantity of each foodstuff should be given to any species, but try to imagine life in the wild where most would not eat every day or all-year round. Encourage activity in predatory herptiles by scattering food – this makes your animal 'work' for its meal. Dragging a defrosted mouse around the vivarium using long tweezers for a snake or releasing some bugs into the vivarium for a Leopard Gecko to physically stalk will aid this type of positive 'exercise'.

Metabolic Bone Disease

This is common in some species of captive-bred reptiles. Without exposure to UVB rays, they cannot synthesize Vitamin D3, which they need to absorb calcium to form healthy bones. There are a variety of products available, and I would advise using a fluorescent full spectrum tube, with both UVA and UVB, or giving a powdered Vitamin D3 supplement.

Abscesses

Common in snakes and lizards, these may appear as a raised bump underneath the scales. A veterinarian can surgically remove the infected swelling and cleanse and suture the wound afterwards.

Dehydration

The symptoms of dehydration are sunken eyes and remnants of unsuccessfully shed skin still attached to the body. Mild cases can be treated by improving your pet's vivarium conditions. Mist spray and make sure the animal drinks. Water bowls can be sunk into the substrate to ground level for ease of access. However, bad cases need veterinarian treatment.

Some moist moss or plants inside this 'hide' assist snakes when they are due to shed their skin by allowing them access to increased humidity.

must know

A terminally sick or aged specimen may need euthanasia. If you think that this is the case with your pet, you must consult a veterinarian.

Improved water quality may have prevented the infection that led to the loss of an eye in this frog.

Sloughing

Maintaining the right humidity levels is key in preventing problems when sloughing. The inability to remove old skin properly can result in a restricted blood supply, especially to blood vessels around toes and fingers. A humidity chamber – a box containing well sprayed plastic plants – is helpful in many species and provides objects for them to rub against to aid the slough. Common problems include:
• A spectacle remaining on a snake – this can be removed carefully with moisture and tweezers by an experienced herpetologist.
• Tattered sloughing in a snake or lizard due to inadequate humidity.

External parasites

These are common problems for reptiles. Mites are pinhead-like objects that run about a reptile's scales, while ticks burrow under the scales, especially near the eyes, nostrils or vent. Good hygiene can help to prevent the problem. Control external parasites with products containing Permethrin. Disinfect the vivarium and furnishings, wash the reptile and treat according to the instructions on the packaging. **Caution**: these products may harm or kill any invertebrate or aquatic animals.

Blisters

These are especially common on Garter Snakes and other species of moist habitats due to the vivarium substrate being too wet or inadequately ventilated. Blisters are also caused by the larvae of nematodes (worm-like parasites). Veterinary treatment is recommended using antiseptic or antibiotics.

Ingested substrate

This causes major problems for many herptiles. Avoid it by providing food in dishes and ensuring feeding animals do not take in any substrate with their food.

Bacterial infections

These are most common in amphibians because of their delicate skin and aquatic lifestyles. Water quality is essential: external or internal filtration is the most effective tool in preventing infection. Dead foodstuffs and faecal matter should be removed by hand or a net regularly. Water bowls must be cleansed and changed, so fresh water is always available.

Salmonellosis

Salmonellosis is an infection caused by contact with the bacteria salmonella. These tiny organisms or germs pass from the faeces of animals or people to other people, foods or animals and cause sickness. Salmonellosis causes diarrhoea, abdominal pains or fever and is usually short-lived, but children and the elderly are susceptible, and it can become a serious health condition requiring antibiotic treatment.

As well as being found in uncooked meats and eggs, salmonella germs are common in pet animals, such as birds and reptiles. If you heed normal animal/human hygiene procedures, e.g. hand-washing with a micro-bacterial solution, never cleaning animal housing or equipment in the same area used for food preparation and disinfecting equipment on a regular basis, you have little to worry about. All pets should be kept clean and well away from kitchens. After any contact with an animal, wash your hands.

want to know more?

• A specialist herptile supplier should be able to offer detailed advice and be knowledgeable about the equipment required to care for these unusual pets. A good shop will stock a wide selection of equipment.
• By using the internet or your local phone book, you should be able to find a supplier near to where you live.

2 Amphibians

Frogs and other amphibians are probably the most colourful pets it is possible to keep. Many hours can be spent watching their behaviour, from the seemingly smiling tree frogs to the antics of an Axolotl or the stalking of a worm by a newt. The vivarium they live in can be planted or otherwise decorated to become a fascinating and attractive feature of any household. Many are kept purely to be enjoyed aesthetically, but others are easy and safe to handle. Keeping any pet has its responsibilities, but amphibians are relatively straightforward to care for, with remarkably simple requirements. They do not need much in the way of day-to-day attention and they can be a joy for their owner.

What are amphibians?

Amphibians ruled the earth before any reptiles, birds or mammals even existed. The word amphibian is derived from the Greek words *amphi*, meaning 'both' and *bios*, meaning 'life'. Amphibians are suited to life on land and in the water and usually have a two-stage life cycle, starting out as aquatic and moving to life on land.

must know

Many amphibians are bred in captivity as pets every year, greatly improving the quality of animals available. Buying a captive-reared juvenile is the best way for you to start keeping, learning about and enjoying these varied, fascinating creatures. A captive-bred frog or salamander will already be adapted to life in a vivarium and more easily conditioned to handling by humans.

Ectotherms

Amphibians have a delicate, moist skin with a protective mucus covering. They slough this periodically, and it is generally eaten. Many display wonderful colours, either for camouflage or as a warning to potential predators to show that they possess toxic skins. Amphibians are ectotherms and are entirely reliant on environmental warmth to maintain their body functions. Most species from temperate climates hibernate in winter to avoid lethally cold temperatures. Species from tropical climates aestivate (pass the summer in a dormant state). Fortunately, in captivity, we can control the environmental conditions, so that they are more suited to year-round activity.

Vertebrates

All amphibians are vertebrates with a complete skeleton from the skull down to tiny toe bones. As adults, all are predators, feeding mainly on spiders and insects, although larger species will consume small reptiles and mammals. Foods are swallowed rather than chewed. To aid this process, frogs, for example, have tiny peg-like teeth to hold the prey before it is swallowed.

Reproduction

Amphibians generally lay soft, jelly-covered eggs in water. Depending on the species these are usually laid in clumps or strings, although some deposit their eggs elsewhere, e.g. on leaves overhanging a pond. Thousands may be laid by each individual, and millions when frogs congregate to breed en masse. However, mortality is high and fewer than one per cent are likely in the wild to reach maturity. The eggs usually hatch into larvae (tadpoles), which, after taking on nutrients, undergo a shape-changing metamorphosis into adult form. They then leave the water and adopt a more terrestrial lifestyle.

The skeleton is the internal frame for all amphibians, and it helps to protect their major organs.

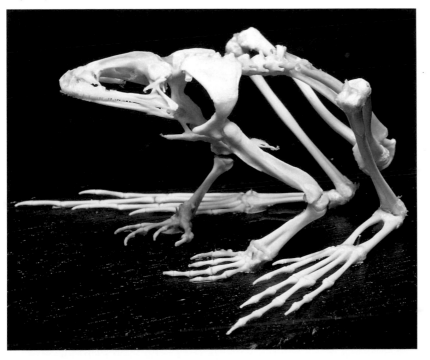

Axolotl *Ambystoma mexicanum*

Found in the wild only in the canal system of the former Lake Xochimilcho in Mexico, these strange amphibians are easy to keep and make attractive, if unusual, aquatic pets. Although officially an endangered species, Axolotls have been available from captive-bred stock since the 1830s.

must know

The Axolotl has been much studied due to its amazing powers of regeneration. A lost or damaged limb will re-grow over a period of about eight weeks. The new limb will be just as good as the old one and full flexibility will be retained. However, occasionally, due to the extent of the original injury, the regenerated limb may re-grow at an unusual angle.

Appearance

Black, or dark grey, is the most common colouring, but albino, harlequin and, more recently, a golden form have all been captive bred and are available to the pet keeper. Growing to 30cm (12in), an Axolotl should live for 10–12 years in captivity, although older specimens of some 20 years have been reported.

Neotony

An unusual feature of Axolotls is that they do not go through a normal amphibian life cycle in which eggs laid in water by the adult hatch into tadpole-like 'larvae' and then metamorphose into adults. At this stage, the animal frequently leaves the water to take up a more terrestrial lifestyle. Axolotls have foregone the need to undergo metamorphosis. They remain in the aquatic larval stage and reproduce without the need to become adult – this is called neotony.

An Axolotl can only change into adult form when the hormone thyroxine is introduced into its diet or there is an increase in the iodine levels in the water. The Axolotl gradually loses its external gills, the tail reduces and, upon leaving the water, becomes a Mexican Salamander. Metamorphosis will not normally take place without this special treatment.

Creating the right environment

A perfect home for a single axolotl is an aquarium
measuring 60 x 38 x 30cm (24 x 15 x 12in). Make
sure that the water is roughly neutral (pH 6.5–7.5)
and is maintained at a temperature of between
10°C (50°F) and 25°C (77°F) – a heater is not usually
required. Water depth can be at least as deep as
the length of your Axolotl, but specimens missing
a limb or two may prefer shallower water until
these have fully regenerated.

Axolotls will soon ruin a delicately planted
aquarium, so they are best kept in a relatively plain
set up or with some sturdier aquarium/pond plants.
Gravel, pebbles and even fine sand are all suitable
substrates. Adding larger rocks will provide visual
appeal to the aquarium and will give your Axolotl
some platforms upon which to rest. An external or

**The long and feathery external
gills allow the Axolotl to obtain
the oxygen it needs.**

This black Axolotl is being carefully lifted to enable its aquarium to be cleaned.

internal filter is recommended to clean and aerate the water but it is not essential. Weekly cleaning of furnishings and partial changes of water is acceptable, although a time-consuming, alternative.

Generally speaking, Axolotls are best housed separately, since they have a tendency to eat each other's limbs. Don't worry if this happens as they do re-grow eventually, if not as perfectly as their originals. Keeping these creatures separately does not usually cause problems, since they seem totally unconcerned about the lack of company.

Handling

Axolotls are aquatic animals and do not like frequent handling. When necessary, they can be moved by scooping them into a net or by gently cradling them in the hands. Always transfer them between waters of similar age and temperature so as not to cause them a shock.

Feeding

Axolotls are predators and will eat a large range of foods. Worms, crickets, small fish, fish pellets that sink or float, cubes of heart or lean meat are suitable foodstuffs. Keep food pieces to small, mouth-sized chunks because Axolotls cannot chew.

A young Axolotl needs 'training' to learn how to catch non-moving food, and long tweezers can be used to drop a piece of food onto its face. They suck their prey in, and this violent motion can scare you from using your own fingers, but their teeth are very fine and will not hurt the more adventurous keeper willing to hold a piece of food between finger and thumb. Axolotls can be fed every other day, with several mouthfuls of food given per sitting. Hungry Axolotls do seem to patrol their environment more than their well-fed companions – an indication that more food may be required. Uneaten food should be removed as soon as possible to minimize fouling.

Breeding

Once your pet is two years old, the sexes can be distinguished easily. Viewed from above, the male Axolotl's head is longer and narrower than the female's, his tail is longer and the swelling at the cloaca is greater.

In captivity, the breeding season coincides with a change of temperature. This can be induced artificially by raising the water temperature to 22°C (72°F) for about a week, and then allowing it to drop quickly. With luck and a good diet, breeding behaviour should follow. The female will become attracted to the male's scent, follow him around the aquarium, and they dance and swim around one another for some time. Eventually the male releases triangular jelly masses, called spermatophores, that sink to the bottom of the aquarium. The female is led over these masses until she takes some up into her cloacal opening. Some hours later she will start to spawn, and 300–600 fertilized eggs are laid.

The egg masses are best reared separately from the parents to prevent them from being damaged or eaten. The eggs need good aeration from a pump. After about two weeks at 20°C (68°F), the larvae will hatch and can then be fed on brine shrimp, tubifex, powdered fish food, or other microscopic foods. As they grow, daphnia, glassworms, bloodworms and mosquito larvae can also be consumed.

must know

When decorating an aquarium for aquatic amphibians, it is important to select rocks, gravel and other furnishings that are suitable from a pet store. Some rocks, stones or pieces of wood found in your garden may in fact be toxic or too sharp for safe use.

Red-spotted Newt *Notophthalmus viridescens*

Native to Eastern North America, these charming and attractive newts make an ideal introduction for novices to the world of tailed amphibians. Easy to maintain, they will grow to a length of 10cm (4in) and live for four to six years.

must know

Red-spotted Newts go through a 'red eft' stage upon metamorphosis. These juveniles are usually red with black dots on their backs and lead a terrestrial lifestyle for two to three years. Once adult, their skin is brown and covered in red spots encircled with a black border. At this stage, they return to the water to live and breed.

These small, attractive newts are easy to keep as pets.

Creating the right environment

The habitat requirements of these newts change as they mature. Metamorphosed juveniles are terrestrial, but adults are mostly aquatic. Several newts may be accommodated in a 60 x 38 x 30cm (24 x 15 x 12in) aquarium, but a larger unit would give you more scope to create a semi-aquatic set up for both stages of the life cycle.

A well-planned vivarium consists of a densely-planted aquatic region, with a water depth of about 15–23cm (6–9in), and a large platform or cork logs stuck or wedged to create a land area. Some sloping branches or rocks provide easy access to the water.

Cover the land area with leaf litter, moss and wood chips to create shelter for both living and hunting. These creatures do not want their habitat to become either too dry or too damp, so aim for humidity of around 40–50 per cent. Fluorescent lighting would help the overall appearance and

also ensure that the plants grow. Do not heat the aquarium – this is important as these newts are content to live with a room temperature of 18°C (65°F) and no higher than 22°C (72°F). An aquarium filter will help maintain good water quality.

Handling
Red-spotted Newts produce toxic skin secretions, making them unpalatable to many predators. Although these toxins will not make you ill, it is always advisable to handle your newts as little as possible. If you do need to handle them, do take care as they are small and easily injured.

Your pet newt will enjoy hunting for food both above and below the surface of the water.

Feeding
Terrestrial efts will hunt small live foods, such as young crickets, waxmoth, fruit flies, worms and spiders. Aquatic adults will hunt daphnia, mosquito larvae and bloodworm, but will also take small food items from the surface of the water. Leave some live foods in the aquarium to allow the newts to hunt at will – but do not overwhelm them.

Breeding
Male Red-spotted Newts actively court the females in the water during springtime. A few weeks after a successful pairing, the female newt will lay up to 400 individual eggs in the aquarium. These will hatch in four to eight weeks, and the tiny larvae begin to feed on suspended micro-organisms for about three months. During this time, they will grow from 1cm (¹/₂in) to 4.5cm (2in) in length and will be ready to undergo their shape-changing metamorphosis.

Paddle-tailed Newt *Pachytriton labiatus*

Paddle tails are an interesting, predatory, tailed amphibian from parts of southern China. Rubbery, chubby and chocolate brown with a bright red streaky belly and flat head, they are very appealing newts. They have a broad, flattened paddle of a tail to help them navigate the fast-flowing streams that make up their habitat in the wild.

must know

Invisible scents called pheromones are produced by the male's cloacal glands, and waft towards a potential mate using the tail. A receptive female will be attracted towards the male who deposits a jelly-like package of sperm (spermatophore). Eventually, often after an elaborate courtship dance, the female will pick up the deposited package directly into her cloacal region.

Creating the right environment

A covered aquarium 90 x 38 x 30cm (36 x 15 x 12in) with some floating 'land' areas is ideal for a small group of these very territorial amphibians. Rocks, real and otherwise, should be utilized to provide multiple hiding and hunting areas for these quite aggressive creatures. A power filter should be considered essential for water purity and to create a current of moving water around the aquarium. Water temperature should remain cool at about 15°C (60°F), so heating is not required. However, a full spectrum light would be helpful for plants and would illuminate the aquarium during the day without raising the water temperature.

Handling

It is best not to pick these animals up but to move them by net or transport them in a small, water-filled fish bag or a moss-filled container. They do breathe air but spend most of their time submerged, coming to the surface of the water only to gulp air or snap at prey.

Feeding

As predators, these newts prefer to hunt living prey around the aquarium; aquatic foods, such as tubifex, blood worm, whiteworm or little freshwater shrimps, are ideal. Small fish, earthworms, crickets, slugs and maggots can all be tried. Variety is important, and any uneaten foods should be removed to minimize fouling the aquatic environment. Paddle tails are little water tigers and will suck in and try to eat whatever takes their fancy.

Newts make fascinating, low-cost pets and their aquarium can be decorated to enhance any room.

Breeding

This is not a species that is widely bred in captivity but it can be achieved if you persist, with good general care of your newts. Males, when in breeding condition, develop several bold white spots on the tail and can usually be identified by their swollen cloaca. Females may lay 40–50 large 4–5mm (¼in) eggs a season that stick to the sides of rocks or caverns. These should hatch after about eight weeks and, if well fed, the tadpoles metamorphose at around two to three months. They may at this stage require a more mossy, land area than a totally aquatic environment.

The rocks and plants in this aquarium have created the ideal environment for a Paddle-tailed Newt. It has lots of places to hide and can climb out of the water if it chooses to do so.

Paddle-tailed Newt | 51

Fire Salamander *Salamandra salamandra*

These secretive creatures are mainly nocturnal, hidden under rocks or inside old rodent burrows during the day. Their natural range extends through central and southern Europe into North Africa and Western Asia. Their bright yellow colouration on an oily black skin is striking and they can grow up to 30cm (12in) long.

must know

Fire Salamanders, like some other amphibians, are very visually aware and will set up 'home' at a regular site. When cleaning out the vivaria, it helps to replace some 'landmark' objects in their original spots so as not to confuse your pets.

Creating the right environment

Fire Salamanders are easy enough to keep but as quite territorial creatures they are best housed individually. A 90 x 38 x 30cm (36 x 15 x 12in) vivarium is spacious for a single animal and sufficient for a pair. Furnish the vivarium with several centimetres of peat, moss and leaves to provide a cool, damp base, add some cork or a small rotting log or something similar to provide hiding spaces. A shallow dish sunk into the ground is useful, but, as salamanders drown very easily, keep it shallow to ensure that your pet can climb out easily. Mist spray your salamanders regularly. Keep them cool at 15–20°C (60–68°F) in low light conditions; supplementary heating or lighting is usually not required.

Handling

The bright colours of the salamander serve as a warning to potential predators. Many creatures learn quickly that these amphibians ooze toxic, milky secretions from their skin when they are bitten or aggravated. Great care should be taken when handling your pet: enjoy your salamander but treat it with respect. A basic hygiene precaution is to wash your hands after touching any animal.

Feeding

If fed at a regular time, your salamander will learn to emerge from hiding in anticipation of food. These terrestrial amphibians eat a range of slow-moving, ground-living live foods, such as slugs, spiders and worms. Be careful when you are feeding several salamanders at once: they are quick to snap and are quite likely to fight over the same worm or cricket. As a simple rule, you should only feed your pet salamander as much as will be eaten at a single sitting, two or three times per week. Without distressing your salamanders too much by leaving excess live food crawling all over them, leave a few worms and insects loose in the vivarium to be eaten or found at their leisure.

Breeding

Fire salamanders are frequently bred in captivity, during spring and early summer. Courtship occurs on land and involves the male carrying the female, often for several hours, on his back. After stimulation of her cloacal region, the female will pick up a deposited spermatophore. At this time, she needs access to shallow water. She will eventually bear up to 70 well-formed larvae direct into the water.

Unlike frogs, all salamanders and newts are deaf and silent, unable to hear, croak or call.

African Clawed Frog *Xenopus laevis*

These amphibians are totally aquatic and are notable for the absence of a tongue and eyelids. Their bodies appear somewhat flattened and they possess powerful hind limbs. They are native to southern Africa and grow to approximately 10–13cm (4–5in). They can live for up to 15 years in captivity.

must know

Clawed frogs really enjoy a variety of foods. Great care must be taken to ensure your Xenopus remains active and fit by eating only enough food to maintain good health. They are prone to obesity and by overeating will become unhealthy and shorten their life span.

Creating the right environment

Simple to maintain in captivity, a 90 x 38 x 30cm (36 x 15 x 12in) aquarium, half filled, is adequate for a pair of frogs. Ideally, the frogs should be able to reach the surface of the water while standing on the bottom of the tank. Keep the water temperature between 20–25°C (68–77°F) with an aquarium heater, making sure that it is adequately protected from damage by these boisterous frogs. To maintain water purity, gentle filtration, using either internal or external power filters, is essential.

To furnish your set up, you can use plants, rocks, pea-sized gravel or even sturdy plants to allow your frogs places to feel secure. A hiding space, such as a plastic pipe, would be much appreciated. Initially, your pets may bash around a fair bit, but they will acclimatize well once familiarized with their new surroundings. Make sure you keep a lid firmly on the aquarium to prevent escapes.

Handling

These frogs are very difficult to handle. Coated with a protected slime, they can easily slip through your fingers. If you need to move them, catch them in a net and transport them in a plastic container, without water, furnished with wet moss or foam pieces to keep them moist. Do not place them in a bag – remember that their claws are sharp and they may rip the bag to pieces.

Feeding

Healthy *Xenopus*, pronounced 'Zenopus', will rarely refuse food, which they shuffle about with their long fingers. They will happily swim to the surface to take food from your fingers, which they will then consume underwater. Earthworms, small fish, waxworms, even turtles and fish food pellets are all agreeable to these frogs.

You should feed only as much as will be eaten in a 10-minute sitting every other day or so. Naturally plump looking, these frogs are prone to gluttony, so keep them healthy.

Breeding

Males and females are easy to tell apart, the female being larger, more rounded and, when viewed from above, having three visible flaps of skin next to the cloaca. Some environmental changes seem to trigger spawning, and spraying the water surface or adding 5–8cm (2–3in) of water can start the process. On average, about 1,000 eggs are laid per spawning, and a single female can produce up to 10,000 a season. These should be removed immediately – to prevent the adult frogs eating them – and should be kept in a shallow container until they hatch a couple of days later. The tadpoles will need an organic soup of microscopic foods that they can suck up. Fish fry food and, indeed, specialist *Xenopus* larvae foods are available.

must know

Popular pets with an unusual appearance, African Clawed Frogs are powerful, agile swimmers with fully-webbed hind limbs that are partially clawed.

The African Clawed Frog, though unusual and bizarre looking, is actually one of the simplest of all amphibians to keep and maintain successfully in the home.

Oriental Fire-bellied Toad *Bombina orientalis*

Splashing around the mountain streams and ponds of Russia, China and Korea is one of the world's most attractive toads. These small, brightly coloured amphibians are active, beautifully marked and very easy to care for. Growing to around 5cm (2in), these charming little creatures can live for up to 20 years.

must know

Oriental Fire-bellied Toads have a bright mossy green back speckled with inky black dots and dashes for camouflage, whilst their underside is an alarmingly reddish-orange, warning of their toxicity to predators.

Creating the right environment

An aquarium/vivarium divided into half land, half water suits these toads. The water part, to a depth of, say, 15cm (6in), can be warmed using an aquarium heater to around 23–25°C (74–77°F); if you live in a colder climate, use a fluorescent light for brightness or a small spotlight. The land area, which needs to be easily reached from the water with branches or rocks helping the toads to climb, should be a moist woodland-type set up with moss, wood chips and leaves for decoration. Alternatively, just keep them in a woodland-type vivarium with a large water bowl. As a semi-aquatic species, water quality is very important.

Active during the day, and small and easy to keep, these entertaining toads make ideal pets.

Handling

Handling these toads is safe but not recommended or, indeed, necessary. Like some other amphibians, Oriental Fire-bellied Toads contain toxins and you should not handle them if you have cuts on your skin. As pets, they are friendly and the release of toxins is rarely seen, so don't let this put you off keeping these delightful toads.

Feeding

These little toads will feed well on live insect prey. They feed mainly on land and will learn to come to your fingers when offered food. Feed as much as they can eat two to three times a week, adding some vitamin supplements regularly. The superb colouration of Oriental Fire Bellies will fade with captive-bred offspring unless colouring agents are provided (found in prepared fish foods and flakes). The toads can obtain these naturally in the wild by eating a multitude of tiny creatures.

Breeding

Spring is the most likely time for these toads to start calling. The male is noisy and his constant 'croaking' should attract a willing female. Spawning will occur within eight to twenty-four hours of mating, probably at night. Up to 200 eggs may be produced singularly or in clumps. Eggs should be removed to a rearing container with similarly aged and warmed water. The 2mm eggs hatch a few days later. Once the larvae have absorbed their egg sacks they will start to eat tiny chopped fish foods and be ready to leave the water (metamorphose) after three weeks as tiny but fully formed toads.

These toads can even be kept communally – a 90 x 38 x 30cm (36 x 15 x 12in) aquarium is ample for three or four individuals (one male to three females). Security is essential, however, as they are excellent escapees.

must know

When threatened, these toads first press their belly to the ground and curl their toes and chins upwards, flashing their bright red undersides to warn of their toxicity. Should you persist in hassling them, they will flip over, exposing the entire red and black belly to deter predators and make themselves appear unpalatable. They can ooze an acrid white fluid from pores on their backs if put under greater stress.

American Green Toad *Bufo debilis*

American Green Toads are very attractive with greenish-yellow metallic looking skin, interlaced with jet black dots and dashes, offering superb camouflage in their natural habitat. Native to arid areas of North America, they are small, squat and undemanding, rarely longer than 5cm (2in) and widely available in pet stores.

must know

Toads are seemingly more intelligent that most other amphibians and, after a period of adjustment to their new home, many soon become tame and comfortable in your presence. In fact, on seeing you approach the vivarium, they are very likely to crawl forward in anticipation of whatever tasty treat you may be about to provide.

Creating the right environment

American Green Toads can be kept happily in pairs or larger groups, provided that ample resting/hiding areas are provided – cork logs and reptile hides are ideal. These toads will thrive in a 60 x 30 x 30cm (24 x 12 x 12in) vivarium with good ventilation and a substrate of compost or sandy soil to a depth of 8cm (3in) or so, as they like to dig in a bit, covered with some leaf litter or moss. A shallow water dish should be available and, although they like a dry woodland-type set up, occasional mist spraying is beneficial and encourages foraging activity.

They thrive in a 20–24°C (68–75°F) temperature range; a heat pad may be useful as back up, or a small spot bulb at one end of a larger vivarium gives toads the option to bask and warm up. A fluorescent light will illuminate the vivarium if required during the day without heating the cage, but ensure that the toads have plenty of shady areas or they may remain hidden until nightfall.

Handling

Toads, as a rule, do not enjoy being handled much and are usually kept by people preferring to marvel at their behaviour, habits and aesthetic appeal.

Feeding

Whilst mainly nocturnal, these and many other toad species thrive in low-light conditions but are likely to become day active (diurnal) once they settle into captivity. They will eat most small live foods that are available from pet stores, including small crickets and small worms.

Breeding

Male American toads have dark grey throats and, in the breeding season, nuptial pads (small dark gripping bumps) on the first digit of the front legs. Females are usually larger with a creamy yellow throat and belly. Native to arid plains and grasslands, these tiny toads breed in the temporary pools of water that are found only after rainfall. Both the eggs and tadpoles develop very quickly to ensure survival once the pools have dried up. In captivity, significant space and effort will be required if you are raising tadpoles into healthy toadlets.

This attractive little toad is secretive but becomes less shy once settled into its vivarium.

Couch's Spadefoot Toad *Scaphiopus couchii*

With large golden eyes, rounded features, yellow to green markings and a creamy white belly, Couch's Spadefoot Toad is an attractive little creature, only reaching about 5-9cm (2-4in) in length. These nocturnal, rotund little amphibians live for around 13 years.

must know

Spadefoot Toads like to dig and, using a special sickle-shaped spade-like structure on each hind limb, create burrows by shuffling backwards into sandy earth. They rest in these burrows and aestivate in them during the harshest months. Couch's Spadefoot is found in the southwest USA and into Mexico and the Baja peninsula.

Creating the right environment

A vivarium measuring approximately 46 x 30 x 30cm (18 x 12 x 12in), or larger if keeping several toads together, will suffice, with a 10-15cm (4-6in) deep substrate of semi-dry sandy soil. Try a 50:50 mix of soil and sand for good burrowing options, although a couple of cave-like retreats on the surface may be preferred. A shallow water dish should always be available. The spotlight or heater pad, controlled by a thermostat, should warm these amphibians to 25-28°C (77-82°F). By using a well ventilated vivarium, an occasional mist spraying will ensure that the toads are warm but do not bake or desiccate in their burrows.

Feeding

Small insects are the preferred diet of these little toads which eat well but may refuse foods for lengthy periods of time. Wild populations reportedly may not eat for eight to ten months of the year, then feast and breed during the very short rainy season. These toads are not hugely active, which, no doubt, assists in keeping them plump with plenty of stored fat. Small crickets are ideal food, but other little live foods should also be offered. such as mini mealworms, waxmoths and earthworms.

Handling

Spadefoot Toads are not good creatures for handling, and some reports suggest that their skin secretions can cause irritation to human skin. If you do need to pick one up, always use wet hands to cup the toad and then move it to a temporary container, as when you are cleaning out the vivarium.

Breeding

During the short, warm rainy season, these toads emerge, and the male's sheep-like bleating call will attract females to the temporary shallow pools of water. Eggs are rapidly deposited and hatch within 36 hours. The tadpoles develop incredibly quickly and can metamorphose within seven to eight days, leaving the water as toadlets before the pool dries up. Tadpoles feed on tiny algae, other tadpoles and undeveloped eggs. If you're breeding them in captivity the toadlets need to be fed tiny crickets and other nutritious insects in order for them to develop into healthy adults.

Although this is a characterful little toad, it is not a species that is recommended for regular handling by pet owners.

Argentinean Horned Frog
Ceratophrys ornate

These strange-looking, spectacularly coloured frogs are shaped like cowpats and are native to the warm, swampy forest floor of Argentina, Brazil, Paraguay and Uruguay. They are variably blotched with mossy greens, yellows and brown pigments, with prominent raised 'horns' behind and above each eye.

must know

An inactive frog with dumpy short legs, it happily spends much of its life burrowed into leaf litter and moss waiting for the next meal to wander by. Horned Frogs are largely diurnal (day active) as pets and grow to 15cm (6in), living usually for about six to eight years, although 15 years has been recorded.

Creating the right environment

Simple to keep, provided that they are kept warm at around 25–28°C (77–82°F) in a set up that can be cleaned easily, these frogs eat well and excrete a lot. They need a mixture of compost/leaf litter with lots of moss for burrowing. This will need regular changing, so keep it simple to maintain good hygiene. A very shallow water dish is essential – the frogs cannot swim – and they may well sit in it for considerable periods of time. Although they are not good pets for someone wanting to watch agile amphibians on the prowl, they are delightful but very lazy slobs, which must be kept alone as they are cannibalistic, territorial and pugnacious.

This giant of a frog is wonderfully colourful and seemingly always hungry. It makes quite a hardy, though inactive, pet.

Handling

This is not a frog to be handled – adults can give you a painful bite, and at any age they will try to eat almost anything that moves. Be warned!

Feeding

Horned Frogs are little more than a stomach on legs and tend to try to eat anything and everything that comes close, including your fingers. This is a frog with an incredible appetite, and, as it grows, more food should be offered. Juveniles will invariably eat crickets, but worms, flies and even small pinkie mice will be accepted. Adults are quite capable of eating other frogs, lizards, snakes and rodents, but, apart from the odd mouse every eight to ten days, most people give them big crickets, worms and locusts. Dead foods are likely to be taken only if wriggled around on long tweezers.

An ambush predator with good camouflage, the Horned Frog will sit and wait patiently for potential food to come towards it.

Breeding

Easy to keep, these frogs thrive in captivity and many are bred in a range of colours. Reaching sexual maturity at two to three years of age, breeding is initiated by the smaller darker males calling for the colourful females during the rainy season. From 300 to 1,000 eggs are deposited on fake or real plants in a shallow water puddle. These hatch within a week or so and require considerable space, filtration and effort to keep them well fed on earthworm, blood worm and tubifex. Even the tadpoles are carnivorous, aggressive and will attack and eat each other as well as small fish. They metamorphose within 30 days into tiny 1–1.3cm ($^1/_2$in) froglets, which are also quite happy to eat each other.

must know

As well as relying on its camouflage for hunting, this frog uses an amazing technique called 'pedal luring' to actively entice food items to venture close. Pedal luring involves wriggling one or more toes to look like a worm, so unsuspecting prey are lured into range of the horned frog's cavernous mouth.

Australian Green Tree Frog *Litoria caerulea*

This wonderful, large green chubby, smiling frog is the most suitable tree frog for the pet keeper. Native to New Guinea and much of Northern and Eastern Australia, they prefer forest but are also common around human habitation. Reaching 5-10cm (2-4in) in length, they live for about 15 years.

These wonderfully robust tree frogs are the easiest to handle amphibian in this book and probably the most popular pet frog in the world.

Creating the right environment

Tall vivaria are required for most tree frogs and these are no exception. A vivarium that measures 60 x 45 x 30cm (24 x 18 x 12in) and is decorated with a branch, plants or logs is ideal for a few frogs. A substrate of moss, bark chips or pebbles is recommended, but a barer base is sufficient and will be much easier to clean.

A large bowl of water should always be offered, and a daily mist spraying is beneficial for the frogs. However, make sure there is a reasonable amount of ventilation to prevent excess dampness. Keep the temperature at 25-30°C (77-86°F) during the day and reduce slightly at night. Only keep similarly sized animals together.

Handling

Australian Tree Frogs are very easy to handle. They climb and stick to your hands quite well, but they may at times leap or jump. When they are first held, they may expel some liquid from their anus. Often assumed to be urine, it is, in fact, only water which the frog absorbs from its water dish in order to keep moist and to provide it with a store of water in case of drought.

Feeding

Australian Green Tree Frogs generally feed on insects, locusts and earthworms but they are also capable of eating vertebrates, such as small frogs and lizards. The occasional pinkie mouse may be offered. Only feed as much as will be consumed over a short period a few times a week. Easy to feed, these frogs enjoy food but they are prone to obesity, so be careful not to over-feed them.

Breeding

After a resting, dry season in the wild, Australian Green Tree Frogs will usually feed, and then, stimulated by the rainfall during the beginning of the onset of the rainy season, they will breed in a few centimetres of water at around 25–30°C (77–86°F). Sometimes this process occurs easily, but an increase in humidity coupled with simulated rainfall may precipitate the spawning.

Between 200 and 2,000 eggs may be laid, and they will hatch within a day or so. If they are fed well on algae and other microscopic particulate foods, these tadpoles will be ready within four to six weeks to metamorphose into tiny froglets.

These frogs may change colour according to the temperature within the vivarium. Individuals of the same size may easily be kept together.

American Green Tree Frog *Hyla cinerea*

Found in the forests and meadows of southern North America, these agile, slender green tree frogs have a distinct creamy white stripe extending from below the eye to the belly. Actively hunting and climbing grasses and bushes, this small 4–6cm (1^1/$_2$–2in) frog is a very visible, attractive vivarium pet.

must know

Most amphibians hibernate to avoid lethally cold winters. Emerging in spring, most species will be eager to breed. In captivity, we replicate this cooling period by gradually reducing the feeding of frogs and their temperature to 5-10°C. Even a few weeks at reduced temperatures will encourage your pets to breed once they are warmed up again. Before trying this for yourself, ask a specialist for more advice.

Creating the right environment

A semi-moist vivarium suits these tree frogs. Height is essential, and several frogs may be housed in a 60 x 46 x 30cm (24 x 18 x 12in) vivarium. During the spring and summer months, a daytime temperature of 18-25°C (65-77°F) is preferred, but this can fall to as low as 12-18°C (54-65°F) at night.

A substrate of wood chips, moss and leaves is superb, and a water dish should be available at all times. Branches or logs will offer opportunities for climbing. Robust plants, e.g. Philodendron, are also excellent, but artificial plants are equally attractive and much easier to maintain in the vivarium.

Avoid using any unprotected lamps or bulbs as leaping frogs can get terribly burnt; fortunately, many vivaria, such as the Exo-Terra range, have mesh screens to prevent such injuries. Heat pads are fine, and full spectrum lighting is excellent.

Handling

American Green Tree Frogs are quite easy to handle, but do ensure that your hands are wet and also remember that the frogs may leap at a moment's notice. These creatures tame relatively quickly and they respond well to hand feeding.

Breeding

These frogs are most likely to breed after a period of over-wintering or hibernation, followed by re-housing in larger, wetter surroundings. Their short breeding season occurs around April to May when the males call loudly for mates. After amplexus (the mating embrace), the coupling pair enter the water. Eggs are fertilized by the male as they leave the female's body, and clumps of 100–400 eggs are deposited amongst the water plants. Transfer these to shallow rearing containers where water is filtered, aerated and kept at around 20°C. Several days later, the larvae, or tadpoles, hatch and should be fed on microscopic organisms and fine powdered fish flakes. Metamorphosis takes around a month when the brown and green coloured froglets, measuring 1–2cm (1/2–1in), are ready for a more terrestrial life. These froglets mature at two to three years of age.

Although they are particularly fond of flying insects, Green Tree Frogs will just as happily eat small to medium sized crickets.

Red-eyed Tree Frog *Agalychnis callidryas*

This is among the most stunning and desirable of the tree frogs, with blood-red eyes, orange feet and blue and cream flashes on its sides – only observed when the frogs are on the move. These placid and delicate frogs are frequently bred and kept in captivity.

must know

Tree frogs have evolved remarkable disc-like suckers or pads at the end of each toe, giving them the ability to climb high up into bushes and trees and adhere firmly when jumping after prey or from branch to branch. Microscopic research has shown that the pads are coated with a thin mucus which adheres by wet adhesion, like wet tissue paper on glass.

Creating the right environment

Tall vivaria, measuring 45 x 60 x 30cm (18 x 24 x 12in), furnished with mosses, real plants and branches, provides an excellent home for these frogs, although many breeders maintain them in a more simple, laboratory-style set up. Attaining the correct balance of humidity, temperature and ventilation is important; they prefer 50–80 per cent humidity, and a daytime temperature of 25–30°C (77–86°F), dropping to approximately 20°C (68°F) at night when they become active. A water bowl must be available at all times and should be cleaned every other day because these and other amphibians absorb water into the bladder – dirty water may

One of the most attractive frogs that are available to pet keepers, the Red-eyed Tree Frog is suitable for the more experienced keeper.

often lead to fatal infections. A full spectrum light source benefits most species and encourages good plant growth for naturalistic vivaria.

Handling

These bright green tree frogs are slow-moving and ponderous by nature. They are nocturnal, and when they are at rest during the day their bright colours are completely concealed from view as their feet are tucked into the body and their eyes are closed; they look just like one of the leaves they prefer to rest on. Handle them cautiously, and only when necessary, because their skin is extremely delicate; it is far better to enjoy them visually. If you need to move them, wait until they are at rest on a leaf, then cut it off and place it in a small tub with some air holes – keep moist and warm.

Feeding

Red-eyed Tree Frogs are very keen on flying foods, such as flies and moths, but crickets and other live foods of suitable size can also be offered. Dust the foods with multi-vitamins and feed as much as will be eaten two to three times a week. Some extras can be left in the vivarium to be hunted later.

Breeding

In the wild, these frogs breed in bushes, shrubs and trees that overhang water. Eggs are laid in a frothy mass on leaves, and the tadpoles, on feeling rain, drop from the leaf into the puddles below. To trigger breeding in captivity, try the simulation technique used for the Australian Tree Frogs (see page 65) but with leafy branches for them to climb on.

Growing to only 8cm (3in), this delicate, beautiful frog is best left in the vivarium and only handled with great care when necessary.

want to know more?

● There are many resources to help you to discover more about frogs. Use the internet as a research tool or visit a library for books relating to amphibians.
● Joining a local wildlife group will help you to find out about native species in your area.
● Or visit the Amphibian Conservation website at www.frogs.org.
● Or try herpetological societies, such as www.international-herpetological-society.org

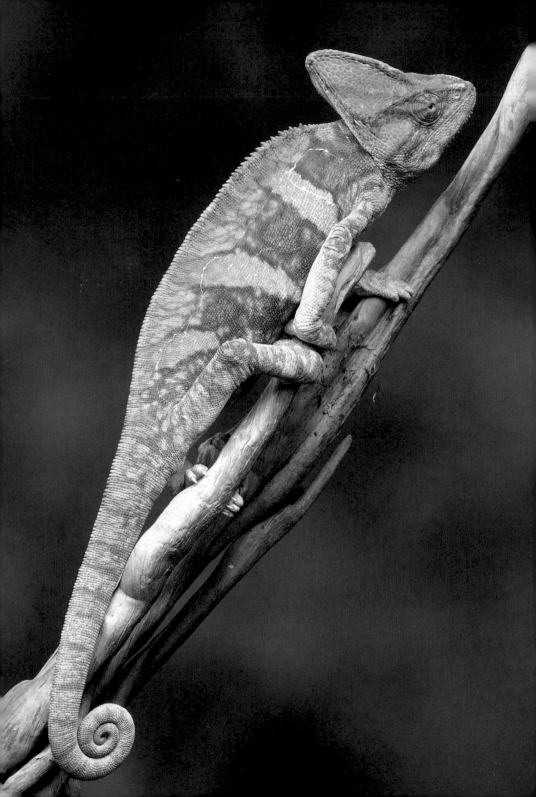

3 Reptiles: lizards and tortoises

Reptiles, including lizards and tortoises, are becoming an increasingly popular choice of pet. From the incredible, colour-changing Chameleon to the endearing Leopard Gecko, these creatures are surprisingly easy to look after. Most lizards are low maintenance, requiring only the occasional feeding and cleaning, and none require walks, annual injections or grooming, but tortoises are more demanding. Other benefits are that lizards and tortoises do not affect asthmatics, make little or no noise and can be kept in a limited space. Moreover, the vivarium your reptile lives in can be decorated like a miniature landscape, adding an attractive feature to your home.

What are reptiles?

Unlike mammals, which utilize food to maintain a steady internal temperature, the temperature of a reptile is dependent on its external environment. Reptiles are often misleadingly referred to as 'cold blooded' animals, but during basking their blood may reach temperatures that are warmer than that of a human.

Lizards and tortoises

Lizards and tortoises are reptiles and they need to bask in the sun or sit upon warm ground when they are cold; conversely, they must retreat into shaded areas if they are to avoid fatal overheating. Their ability to lighten or darken the skin also helps this process – lighter skin reflects heat whereas darker skin absorbs it.

Reptile skin is effectively watertight because it is covered by protective scales. In some species, like the tortoise, these scales are enlarged and contain bony plates which, along with flattened and fused vertebrae, form the shell. The skin of reptiles may appear shiny but is never slimy, and after shedding is usually eaten. All lizards are vertebrate animals with an internal skeleton, from the brain-protecting skull right down through the spine, ribs and tail bones to the (apart from legless species) tiny leg and toe bones.

Species of lizards

Over 3,500 species of lizard are known and, although they are bound by common characteristics, there is considerable variation in their diet, habitat, and behaviour. Most species are predators, eating rodents,

There are at least 3,500 species of lizard discovered so far of which only a few are suitable as pets. Herpetology is the study of both reptiles and amphibians.

amphibians and insects, but some consume both plant and animal matter (omnivores), and a few are entirely herbivorous, existing on fruits, flowers and leaves. Many are solitary by nature, congregating only to breed, although some exhibit complex family or group dynamics.

Egg layers

The majority of lizards and all chelonia (tortoises and turtles) are egg layers. Eggs may be deposited into leaf litter, buried in a hole dug in the ground or even stuck to tree bark or vegetation. Some eggs have a hard shell whereas others have a leathery, parchment-like texture. Once eggs are laid, they are incubated by environmental warmth alone. Reptile young are always born, or hatch, as miniature replicas of their parents – no metamorphic stage exists as it does in amphibians.

This tortoise is one of a huge number of reptiles now bred in captivity as pets, ensuring that high-quality animals are available without affecting wild populations.

Leopard Gecko *Eublepharis macularius*

Unlike most members of the *Gekkonidae* family, these striking and attractive geckos are not noted for their climbing abilities as they lack the 'adhesive' pads on their digits. They are ground dwelling and have small sharp claws.

An excellent introduction to reptile keeping, this attractive lizard is a popular choice for the inexperienced pet keeper.

Natural habitat

Spotted like the big cat that shares their name, these geckos are terrestrial and adapted to life in the harsh, arid rocky deserts of northwestern India, Pakistan, Iran and Iraq. Living alone or in small groups, they avoid the fatally hot daytime by hiding under rocks and boulders. The fully grown adults measure around 20–22cm (8in) in length, and these pretty yellow-and-mauve reptiles can live for up to 30 years as pets.

Creating the right environment

Ideally, your Leopard Gecko should be housed separately, where there is no competition for food or for shelters. A 60 x 30 x 30cm (24 x 12 x 12in) vivarium will provide ample space for a single specimen. Larger vivaria, such as 90 x 60 x 30 cm (36 x 24 x 12in), would be suitable for a trio of geckos – all females or two females and one male – and gives you the creative opportunity to make an attractive desert-like set up for your pets.

If a temperature range of 27–32°C (80–88°F) is maintained and your set up provides the essentials of food, water and shelter, your gecko should thrive. A heater pad is all that is required to ensure adequate warmth. By placing it at one end of the vivarium,

All pet Leopard Geckos are bred in captivity and are available in a wide variety of colours and patterns.

your pet can warm up or cool down (thermoregulate) as it wishes. Coir chippings, pea gravel and wood chips – or just some paper – can be used as a base or substrate. Live succulents and other 'house' plants can be added to good decorative effect: simply bury the pot in some substrate well away from the heat source and don't forget to water the plant. A piece of driftwood is also highly effective and will give your gecko something to climb on.

Clean creatures
Geckos are very clean creatures and will select and use a toilet site. Their droppings dry quickly, and they should be removed on a regular basis. Even in groups, most vivaria will require a complete clean out only once every few months.

must know

Most reptiles benefit hugely from the addition of a humidity chamber somewhere in the vivarium. A pile of plastic plants or some real moss, regularly mist sprayed and enclosed in a box that your lizard can enter at will, is very useful to prevent dehydration and helps to facilitate periodic skin shedding.

Feeding

Leopard Geckos should be fed every other day or so. They can consume most small to medium live foods, such as crickets, a few of which should be placed within the vivarium for your lizard to stalk as desired. Being nocturnal, most feeding will occur overnight. Water, replaced regularly, should always be available in a shallow dish on the ground, and occasional mist spraying is enjoyed and beneficial.

Handling

Leopard Geckos tolerate handling well, although it is best to sit down when handling any reptile in case it is dropped or jumps out of your hand. The best time to start taming your lizard is while it is still young. Handle it for short, regular periods to show your pet you pose no threat to its safety.

Handling from an early age will ensure your Leopard Gecko grows into a tame and friendly adult.

Breeding

Leopard Geckos breed well in captivity. Mating usually occurs unseen in a covered area, and the first signs of a successful coupling is the female's noticeably swollen belly. Each female can lay several clutches of two eggs per year. Try to encourage her to lay her eggs in a suitable spot – an upturned plastic container, with a hole cut in one side and filled with moistened vermiculite, is ideal.

The two eggs, being a standard clutch for most geckos, should be transferred to an incubator to prevent desiccation. Unlike many bird eggs, reptile eggs should not be turned – simply place them in the incubating medium and cover. Provide airflow but keep humidity at 70–80 per cent and maintain a temperature of 30°C (86°F).

The incubating eggs should be checked on a regular basis – very shrivelled or mouldy ones should be removed to avoid contaminating healthy eggs. A white but slightly indented egg needs a higher humidity level. The young will hatch after six to twelve weeks. The juveniles are marked with yellow and black bands that will gradually break up into the familiar adult markings. They should be housed in small rearing containers, separately if possible. If kept communally, you must provide several hiding places and water dishes, removing the more dominant individuals once they begin to harass others. A daily misting will ensure good skin condition and ease frequent shedding as the juveniles grow. Small crickets and waxworms are ideal first foods – geckos also adore small spiders. All foodstuffs should be lightly dusted with a multi-vitamin and mineral supplement.

must know

A Leopard Gecko sheds, or sloughs, its skin on a regular basis as it grows. The peeling skin is fine and translucent and the lizards normally eat it. Probably nutritious, by eating it predators are less likely to detect a gecko's presence. Your lizard fades in colour as the shedding begins. A new more colourful skin is revealed as the old one is consumed. Some species, such as Blue-tongued Skinks, simply leave the skin behind and wander off.

Peacock Day Gecko *Phelsuma quadriocellata*

Delightful little jewels, Peacock Day Geckos can make a vivarium come alive with flashes of colour as they patrol their territory. Compared to other Day Geckos, this spotted variety is a dwarf species reaching only 7.5cm (3in) in length.

must know

Whereas most geckos are nocturnal and somewhat dull in colour, Day Geckos are active by day and the most flamboyant members of the *Gekkonidae* family. Day geckos have no moveable eyelids and use their tongue to wipe clean and moisturize their eyes.

Habitat and appearance

Day Geckos are found on islands in the Indian Ocean – Madagascar, Mauritius and the Seychelles. The Peacock Day Gecko has a peacock-like eye marking on either side of the body behind the front legs, red spots and blobs on the back and a vivid 'V' on its face.

Creating the right environment

A 50 x 30 x 60cm (20 x 12 x 24in) vivarium is really only suitable for a single lizard. Males should either be housed individually or one male with several females. With larger vivaria, it is much easier to create a suitable environment for a harem of lizards to enjoy – without adequate space, food or basking opportunity, some individuals could be bullied. A maximum temperature of 32°C (88°F) should be maintained during the day, which can fall at night to a cooler 20–22°C (68–72°F).

Handling

Day Geckos are virtually impossible to hold, so enjoy them for what they are, lovely creatures bounding around their vivarium. Should you need to transport or move one, place a clear plastic tub over it and slide a piece of card underneath to contain the lizard.

Feeding

Day Geckos are small arboreal lizards and only little foods are suitable – small crickets, waxmoth larvae and flies are relished. Live foods can be dusted with vitamin and mineral supplements as recommended. Whilst essentially insectivores, their habit of licking fruit is well known, and small chunks of sweet fruits, such as mango or grape, and honey or jam are enjoyed. Mist spraying morning and night should keep humidity levels high in glass vivaria.

Breeding

Once Day Geckos are happily housed in a vivarium, breeding is sure to follow. Day Geckos, unlike most other reptiles, lay hard calciferous eggs, which in most cases adhere to almost any surface, from the glass or wooden side of the vivarium to a bamboo pole. Don't try to cut or remove them, but ensure that the eggs are warmed sufficiently to incubate successfully just where they are.

must know

A well-balanced planted vivarium can look great with Day Geckos leaping from leaf to leaf. Broad-leaved plants, such as Mother-in-laws tongue, philodendrons and Sanservia are very effective. Bamboo poles make great basking areas placed safely away from, but in reach of, the bulb's rays. Ground substrate is not really needed, so lizard grass is one option, or leaf litter and wood chips or coir.

Standing's Day Gecko *Phelsuma standingi*

These large Day Geckos grow up to 25cm (10in) in length and can live for up to 10 years in captivity. Native to a restricted range in parts of southwestern Madagascar, they inhabit more arid, thorny forests than the lush, densely planted areas favoured by most Day Geckos.

must know

The only home for Standings Gecko may soon be in captivity as their natural habitat is disappearing very fast. Forests and scrubland are cleared for agriculture and other developments that benefit mankind, and over 75 per cent of Madagascar's natural forests are long gone already. By keeping and learning about these lizards, we may help a species that is sadly likely to disappear in the wild.

Creating the right environment

Like all Day Geckos, very little time is spent on the ground, so you can dispense with ground coverings or substrate. You can line the cage with newspaper for ease of cleaning, but large pebbles or natural décor like bamboo are more attractive. A pair or trio (one male and two females) can be housed spaciously in a 60 x 60 x 60cm (24 x 24 x 24in) vivarium. Whilst mist spraying is needed for drinking, this species seems to prefer slightly higher, more steady temperatures of about 32°C (88°F) and lower humidity (70-75 per cent) than other Day Geckos. At night, as temperatures drop to around 18-22°C (65-72°F), they will sleep on leaves or in a sheltered piece of tree bark.

Handling

Day Geckos are not an easily handled species and are best kept to observe and enjoy as the colourful creatures they are. For advice on transporting or moving a Day Gecko, see page 79.

Feeding

Large Day Geckos can eat most insects available to the enthusiast. Beetle grubs and crickets are relished, and most foodstuffs should be regularly dusted with vitamin/mineral supplements to ensure optimum health. Sweet fruits and nectar are best offered high up in the vivarium on tiny bottle tops or upturned jam-jar lids. Food can be offered at feeding stations by placing insects in suspended plastic pet homes that the lizard can reach at will, but from which the insects cannot escape. 'Take away' food insects will need pieces of orange or apple to ensure that they too can eat and drink. For water, mist spray, but this gecko will learn to drink from a shallow dish placed high within the vivarium rather than at ground level.

Breeding

Females, upon maturing, are easily sexed by the calcium deposit bulges on their necks, which can grow alarmingly large but are entirely natural. Males have a more slender neck and frame and 'V'-shaped indented preanal pores on their undersides. Eggs hatch after 50–60 days, sticking together in one or two batches in the vivarium on glass or bamboo. A pair may produce eggs for around six months of the year but need to be well fed with nourishing food to sustain this rate of production. Females will not only guard their eggs but also protect baby Day Geckos for several months after hatching.

Although patterns and colours vary in this species, these geckos tend to have sky-blue skin and green heads with black, crazy-paving, net-like patterns.

Giant Day Gecko *Phelsuma madagascarensis*

These stunning lizards are easy to keep and breed. Their skin is an electric lime green and they can have, depending on the exact sub species, orange-red markings in the form of dots or blobs along the back and between the nostrils and eyes. Active by day, these large geckos can reach 25cm (10in) in length.

must know

Day Geckos are very fond of sweet fruit and plant saps. A halved grape, positioned securely high in the vivarium, will attract a gecko for a prolonged licking session. Licking foods no doubt provide essential minerals and vitamins for these sweet-toothed lizards.

The tiny suction pads on geckos' toes enable them to grip and climb even the smoothest surface.

Creating the right environment

A planted vivarium will make the most attractive display for these pretty geckos. A huge range of 'house plants' available from garden centres are suitable, but amongst the easiest to maintain are philodendrons, ficus, yuccas, hoya, oleander and passion flower. The use of full spectrum lamps will assist both your plants and your lizards in growing and developing naturally. However, you must ensure that growing plants do not interfere with the heating or lighting equipment. Artificial plants are just as effective and come without any maintenance issues, apart from washing.

In the vivarium, replicate a tropical temperature range of 25–32°C (77–88°F). These lizards enjoy humidity levels reaching 80 per cent, so mist spray or add a reptile water feature. Fresh air is greatly appreciated and you should always keep your vivarium well ventilated.

It is best to keep these territorial geckos singly or in a harem of one male to two or more females if space is available. A 60 x 60 x 60cm (24 x 24 x 24in) vivarium is ample for two to three individuals, while 60 x 45 x 30cm (24 x 18 x 12in) is fine for a solitary gecko; the bigger and taller the vivarium the better.

Handling

You are very unlikely to ever handle a Giant Day Gecko. If they are physically restrained, you will risk tearing their delicate skin and they are far too active to sit still on you.

Feeding

The majority of food eaten by these lizards is insect matter, and both crawling and flying foods are taken with gusto. They love to drink from droplets, so do spray regularly to ensure that they do not get thirsty. They will soon learn to use a water feature.

Breeding

If geckoes are kept in adult groups, breeding is likely. Look out for the typical clutch of two hard-shelled eggs of 1cm (^{1}/$_2$in) across. Leave in the vivarium to hatch – hopefully, the female will have deposited them where the temperatures of around 25–30°C (77–86°F) will incubate them in around 45–60 days.

This muscular lizard looks in excellent health. Day Geckos do not have moveable eyelids and keep their large eyes clean with regular licks from the tongue.

Green Anole *Anolis carolinensis*

Anoles are charming small lizards and a popular choice of pet. They leap and dart about, providing you with hours of visual entertainment. Active during daylight hours, the males are highly territorial and aggressive to one another, signalling with bright flashes of colour from their throat fans or dewlaps.

must know

Sometimes called American Chameleons, Anoles are native to the southern United States, Central America and the Caribbean, where they can be found on walls, fences and shrubs in gardens and other man-made settlements. Green Anoles measure 13-20cm (5-8in) in length and can live for three to five years.

Creating the right environment

Anoles will thrive in a tall vivarium with either real or replica plants and branches. A harem of four females to one male is about the best ratio for a community set up in a vivarium measuring at least 90 x 60 x 30cm (36 x 24 x 12in). You can minimize competition for the 'best' basking spot by offering two or more options. A temperature range of 24-30°C (75-86°F) is ideal, and full spectrum lighting will assist both the healthy development of lizards and plants. Night-time temperatures can safely drop to 20°C (68°F).

This species really appreciates humidity as well as fresh air. Regular mist spraying will assist, but adding a water feature, dripper or mister will help raise humidity levels generally.

Handling

Although fast and able to leap about, an Anole will learn to sit on your hand in exchange for a tasty treat. These small and delicate lizards need a gentle touch and allowing one to climb onto your hand is less stressful for the animal. If you wish to move your pet, grip it firmly but gently. This is a lizard that is much better for observing than handling.

Feeding

These insectivores will eat any small to medium live insect foods. Mealworms should be avoided as many will pass through them undigested. Feed at least twice weekly, watching to ensure that every occupant gets several insects per feeding. A small surplus amount of live food may be present in the vivarium at all times. Mist spraying once a day or so is essential, as Anoles prefer to drink water droplets from leaves rather than still water from a bowl. Alternatively, consider a drip system or mister.

Breeding

Once you establish a group of these lizards and they are well fed and happy, breeding is sure to follow. One or two eggs are laid about a fortnight after mating. These will be buried by the female, pushed by her nose into the compost in a warm and damp area, frequently either around the pot or roots of a climbing plant, such as Philodendron. The tiny baby Anoles will need equally tiny fruit flies and micro crickets to start feeding on.

Adult male Anoles are more brightly coloured than females, and only males display using their colourful throat fans, or dewlaps accompanied by head bobbing.

Blue-tongued Skink *Tiliqua sp.*

Skinks are a widespread family of lizards found around the globe in both temperate and tropical areas. Over 1,200 species are known to science, but few are as attractive or as easy to keep or breed as the magnificent Blue-tongue.

must know

As the name suggests, these lizards have a lovely big blue tongue. If threatened, this can be flattened and rippled inside an open mouth which, accompanied by a hiss, acts as an effective deterrent to would-be predators.

Appearance and habitat

These stocky 50cm (20in) lizards have overlapping scales and can be found on the ground in Australia and Tasmania where they live amongst leaf litter, consuming invertebrates and snails as well as fruit – many live underground. New species of skink are still being discovered, but they all have certain characteristics in common. Skinks are noted for their long flattened, shiny bodies and degenerate or reduced limbs – some are completely limbless while other types have very small and very weak legs.

Most skinks are omnivorous and, including the Blue-tongue, give birth to live young, rather than lay eggs. They may live for 10–15 years. Juvenile skinks are particularly vulnerable to introduced predators, such as cats in Australia, and are diminishing in numbers right across their range.

Creating the right environment

Blue-tongued Skinks should be kept singly as a rule as they can be very aggressive towards one another. A dry, woodland type of habitat is ideal for this totally terrestrial species. The ground can be covered in cork logs for retreats and decorated for visual effect with leaf litter, twigs and mossy rocks. Remember that these lizards root around under ground debris looking for food, and therefore a delicately planted vivarium would be quickly ruined.

A vivarium for a single skink should measure at least 120 x 30 x 30cm (48 x 12 x 12in) with a daytime temperature gradient of 25–35°C (77–95°F), falling at night to 18–20°C (65–68°F). The combination of a heater pad at one end and a thermostatically-controlled spotlight, wired up to a timer switch, will warm the tank and create a daytime basking area. Timing the light to switch off during the evening would automatically reduce the temperature. Full spectrum lighting is generally recommended for successful long-term care and breeding, but any exposure to natural sunlight outside is a good thing. Many people keep this species in outdoor enclosures when it is warm enough, but ensure they cannot escape and are safe from predators.

Young captive bred Blue-tongues are normally acquired when they are about a couple of months old. With regular handling, they can become very tame.

Handling

The temperament of lizards can vary, just like people, but for many years the Blue-tongue Lizard has been considered a good choice for close contact. They are normally very tolerant of handling and quite enjoy a stroke or scratch. Their small claws may feel sharp on younger hands and they always need to feel supported under their body and legs.

Feeding

My Blue-tongued Skinks enjoy variations of the diet that is described below, but they can easily become obese, so take care not to feed them every day.

must know

The skin of lizards varies enormously but is based upon the 'scale' in all species. Blue-tongued Skinks have tough, almost armoured, scales for rummaging in the Australian bush. Scales are made of keratin, a fibrous structural protein, which is also a component of nails, hair, horns and feathers.

These scavenging omnivores enjoy a huge range of vegetables, fruits and flowers.

A large batch of food can be prepared at one time and then frozen in small portions for later use. Mango, apple, banana, berries, salad leaves and peas, for example, can be finely chopped and then mixed with a little dog food or minced beef, much to the lizard's satisfaction. Snails are also relished, the shell being crunched and then spat out. A good balance to aim for is roughly 70 per cent greens and fruit to 30 per cent meat.

Offer your pet fresh food three or four times a week in a shallow dish; uneaten foods should be removed within a few hours. Pinky mice are also easy and nutritious foods. Water should be available to drink and these lizards will love a mist spray. The moist conditions will stimulate them to emerge and look for their food. They are particularly keen to feed after shedding their skin.

Popular medium-sized lizards, these impressive skinks are easy to maintain and enjoy a variety of readily available foodstuffs.

Breeding

Producing between six and twenty live young once a year, Blue-tongue Skinks can be quite a prolific species. Breeding is possible at two to three years with adult lizards introduced in spring after a cooling-off period. Males grab and bite females around the neck before mating takes place.

Sexing

When mating is observed, this is probably the only time you can reliably tell the male from the female. Sexing is not at all easy but females will tend to have a broader body, while males may just show signs of penile bulges at the base of the tail when viewed from underneath. These are live-bearing lizards and worth the effort to breed.

must know

Blue-tongued lizards are the largest members of the skink family. Seventeen species are recognized, most occurring in Australia where, being terrestrial and solitary, they spend much their time either at rest or foraging under vegetation on the ground.

Bearded Dragon *Pogona vitticeps*

A remarkable Australian native, the Bearded Dragon is noted for its ease of care and good temperament, living to around 10 years old. In the wild, these Dragon lizards are equally at home in lush suburban gardens or the more open and hot desert.

Dragon lizards are dramatic and active vivarium pets.

Appearance

Diurnal and 40–60cm (16–24in) in length, this is an omnivorous reptile. Medium sized but heavy bodied, their name in part comes from their extendible beard. The back, head and tail are rough to the touch, whilst the belly is white and soft. Along both sides of the body runs a line of fine long spines which help camouflage the lizard by breaking up its visible outline when it presses against the branch of a tree.

Creating the right environment

A dry woodland or desert-style vivarium is suitable for these lizards. A unit measuring 90 x 50 x 90cm (36 x 20 x 36in) is suitable for an adult pair or trio (two females and one male). Two young Beardies would need at least a 60 x 30 x 30cm (24 x 12 x 12in) vivarium for the first few months of their life. Unless you intend to breed them, it is best to house and keep them alone, or to keep only females together as males become quite territorial.

Provide cork logs or rocks for climbing on or burrowing under, and cover the vivarium floor with bark chips or play sand. If two or more Beardies are kept together, several basking areas must be provided to minimize competition. Temperatures can reach as high as 40°C (104°F) at the basking end of their set up, but can reduce to 20°C (68°F) at night. Heater pads are useful to ensure that an area of substrate is warm and dry at all times, and full spectrum lighting is essential for healthy growth and development.

A clean shallow dish of fresh water should always be available for drinking, and your Bearded Dragon will enjoy an occasional mist spraying or supervised bath. Soiled areas need regular cleaning.

Handling

These lizards tame very quickly while they are still young. Regular handling at this stage should ensure that your lizard remains willing to be handled. They are very unlikely ever to try and bite you. If unwilling to be picked up, they will usually just walk or jump away.

Feeding

These are omnivorous lizards with a good appetite; they are prone, if anything, to overeating. A well-supplemented diet is recommended, especially for

Young Bearded Dragon lizards tame very easily when they are frequently handled by keepers.

must know

Bearded Dragons try to retain their original tail , but the end may be bitten off by an aggressor. Some lizards will use 'autonomy' for defence: the tail breaks off but keeps on wriggling to divert the aggressor. In time, a new tail grows back. Other lizards use their tail as a weapon or whip, or to store fat.

An adult Bearded Dragon in relaxed pose. When threatened, it will puff up its spiky beard from which it derives its name.

the fast-growing juveniles. A vast range of food types may be offered, including commercially farmed insects, some processed dried lizard foods and pink mice for their nutritional value. Plant material, such as spring greens, dandelion flowers and leaves, are relished and should be chopped for smaller individuals to manage easily.

A well-defined social hierarchy develops within any group of Bearded Dragons, and at feeding time it is interesting to observe their behaviour. The largest or most dominant lizard will feed first, the others waiting and watching with their tails clearly bent upwards, signalling their lowly status.

Only after the dominant lizard has finished his meal and moves away do the other subordinate lizards get their chance to feed. If keeping a group of Dragon lizards, it is essential to provide ample basking sites and adequate food, so that all the members of your family group can thrive.

Breeding

Bearded Dragons become sexually mature between their first and second years. Both sexes have spines on the head, neck and throat, but only males develop the coal-black throat and tail tip during courtship, or when involved in ritualistic fighting over territory. This will be accompanied by much 'head-bobbing'. A healthy female may lay six clutches of eggs in a season, averaging 20 eggs per clutch. These are buried deep into the soil – up to 20cm (8in) – or into a laying box containing vermiculite. They need to be incubated at 29°C (84°F) for about 60 days. After producing eggs or live young, herptiles benefit from a period of isolation and a nutrition-packed diet in order to recover adequately for future breeding.

Females either lack or have much less prominent pores around the thighs or anal area.

Sexing a lizard

Lizards usually have visual characteristics that make it easy to sex them. Most lizards can be easily sexed by the time they are one year old. It helps to have several individuals of the same age to compare the differences. The following guidelines should help.

1 Most, but not all, male lizards are larger and stronger looking than females.

2 Males usually have thicker and longer tails than female lizards.

3 Males have larger more colourful dewlaps, bigger head crests and even horns.

4 Females lack entirely or have less prominent pores around the cloacal area or on the thighs. To examine these, hold the lizard firmly and then turn it upside down. They look just like ordinary scales but are often marked with a dimple and clearly visible in a 'V' shape just above the anal opening.

Males usually have thicker and longer tails than females and more noticeable pores. Maturing male beardies are easily sexed by their extendible black beard.

Veiled Chameleon *Chameleo calyptratus*

Chameleons are unlike any other lizards and are a favourite choice for anyone who is interested in fantastic reptiles. Also called the Yemen Chameleon, this lizard is native to Saudi Arabia and Yemen.

must know

This species is captive bred in large numbers and would appear to be one of the most adaptable chameleon species for the pet keeper willing to invest some time and effort. With a two-to-eight-year life span, these are short-lived lizards and grow up to 33cm (13in) for females and up to 6ocm (24in) for males.

Creating the right environment

Like many lizards, chameleons like furnishings in the vivarium to remain in the same place, so place plants, branches or watering areas in permanent sites. Chameleons are best housed in larger vivaria: a single specimen needs a 90 x 90 x 50cm (36 x 36 x 20in) vivarium and a daytime temperature of 20–30°C (68–86°F). Like most lizards, the males are solitary and very aggressive, so they are best kept singly.

As chameleons are bush or shrub dwellers, offer living plants or, at least, sturdy plastic plants and branches on which to climb. Position spotlights that create basking areas away from live or plastic plants as they may singe or melt. Full spectrum lighting will ensure good plant and pet growth. Mist spray daily and/or provide a circulating water feature to keep humidity levels up. Do make sure there is good ventilation without causing chilly draughts.

Handling

Most Veiled Chameleons tolerate handling relatively well, especially if it involves hand feeding. Start while your pet is quite young to condition it to this sort of contact on a regular basis. Never pick up the chameleon as this causes great offence and visible stress. Instead, allow it to climb up onto your hand and fingers or a small hand-held branch.

Feeding

Chameleons need to eat and
drink regularly, with water being
preferred in droplet form. All live foods can be
tried, but climbing or flying insects are best. Vary
the diet to provide a range of vitamins and minerals.
Some garden-caught food is advised, and larger
Veiled Chameleons may accept highly nutritious pink
mice. This lizard will also eat a range of leaves, fruit
and vegetables. These and, indeed, all foods should
be dusted with vitamin and mineral supplements.

**The fascinating Veiled Chameleon
is easy to keep and the most
commonly bred chameleon species.**

Breeding

These lizards are prolific egg layers, and a female
may lay clutches numbering between 25 and
80 eggs, three to four times a year. This productivity
does take its toll eventually and females rarely
survive much beyond their fifth clutch. The eggs
are buried in soil or sand and should be placed in
vermiculite and incubated at 27–29.5°C (80–85°F)
during the day, with a small night-time drop in
temperature to 24°C (75°F). Juvenile chameleons
grow rapidly and it is in these first crucial months
that a varied and well-supplemented diet will
enable them to grow up into healthy, mature
specimens. They need a larger range and variety
of insect prey than the adults, which tend to enjoy
a more omnivorous diet. Growing fast, they need
to be separated within 10–12 weeks.

Panther Chameleon
Chameleo pardalis (now officially Furcifer pardalis)

These large colourful lizards are well worth the extra care that is required to ensure success within the vivarium. Native to Madagascar, they can also be found on a few neighbouring islands, such as Mauritus and Reunion, where they have been introduced to control pest insects on plantations.

must know

Entirely diurnal, these short-lived creatures have a lifespan of around two to three years and they range in size from 33cm (13in) for females to 51cm (20in) for males.

Appearance
Probably the most incredible lizards of all, chameleons are a true wonder of the natural world. They are noted for their many unusual features: they have amazing colour changing abilities, independently moving eyes and an incredible, extendible tongue. The chameleon's amazing ability to change colour is much misunderstood. Emotions and territorial posturing, as well as camouflage, are responsible for the array of colours exhibited. Chameleons are very desirable as pets.

Creating the right environment
Unless a large enclosure is available for a pair or trio (two females to one male), Panther Chameleons are best kept singly. Males are very territorial and will fight and injure one another if kept together, but if housed alone they appear to be easier to keep and are of less nervous disposition than the females. I would recommend a minimum 60 x 60 x 60cm (24 x 24 x 24in) vivarium for juveniles or solitary individuals, but the optimum size would be 60 x 180 x 60cm (24 x 72 x 24in), the greater height giving more scope to create an attractive set up.

A temperature gradient of 26–35°C (78–95°F) is ideal, and full spectrum light is essential unless regular exposure to natural sunlight is available. Panther Chameleons cannot tolerate temperatures lower than 20°C (68°F) and must always be warm. Do remember, however, never to place your vivarium near a window to provide extra sunshine for your pet. The useful ultraviolet rays will not penetrate glass or plastic anyway and may well turn your vivarium into an oven with direct sunlight lifting the temperature to a fatally high level.

One or more spotlights are best used to create a basking area, and you may consider ceramic heaters for cooler nights. Provide branches and plants, real or plastic, for your pet to climb on but try to keep them in the same places – lizards like familiarity.

Humidity and ventilation

These chameleons prefer a higher humidity for at least part of the day – around 75 per cent. They also prefer to drink from droplets on leaves. Compared to other lizards, they do tend to drink a lot of water and inhabit areas in the wild with high rainfall and moisture. Conditions must not get stale within the vivarium, so good ventilation and fresh air are key. A small fan can help circulate and freshen the air but it must always be placed out of reach of the vivarium's inhabitants.

Male Panther Chameleons are more colourful than the females, and may be green, red, orange, lemon or even turquoise.

The Chameleon's foot is uniquely adapted to its climbing lifestyle; as seen above, its opposing toes provide an excellent grip.

The chameleon's skin contains many chromatophores (pigment-filled cells) which enable rapid change in skin colouration.

Handling

Some chameleons will tolerate handling by their keepers relatively well, especially if it involves hand feeding. Start handling your pet when it is still quite young to condition it to this kind of contact on a regular basis. Never pick up a chameleon, but, instead, allow it to climb up onto your hand and fingers. If permitted to do so, it will continue to climb until it reaches your shoulders and head.

Feeding

Panthers are insectivorous, eating almost any live foods and the odd pinky. Flying or climbing insect prey is preferred, and variety is the key to providing vitamins and minerals for healthy development. Chameleons like, and need, quite a lot of food, but there is less risk of obesity with these lizards than other species. They drink more than other reptiles,

must know

The chameleon's tongue is a complex but highly effective hunting tool. It is like a long, hollow tube, along the length of which runs a powerful muscle that can be expanded or relaxed at will. Each expansion shoots the tongue out from its anchor point in the floor of the mouth. The tip of the tongue is bulbous and coated in tacky secretions designed to hold the prey firmly whilst the tongue recoils back into the mouth. Each eye is capable of moving independently and of judging distance. The chameleon can then 'shoot' with its tongue with deadly accuracy – but don't blink; it all happens incredibly quickly.

preferring droplets to still water in a bowl. Mist spray daily and/or provide a water dripping system.

Live foods
One method of supplying live foods without insects dispersing into the vivarium is to attach an opaque pet home, or similar steep and smooth-sided bowl, to a feeding branch. This will position food within the range of the chameleon and its tongue, without enabling the bugs to reach the branch to escape. Make sure the bug home is well stocked and the bugs are well fed – the chameleon will use this 'service station' for a top up.

Breeding
About a month after a successful mating, the female will lay 20–30 eggs, which are typically chameleon: white, oval and parchment-like in appearance. These will be buried in the egg-laying material that should already have been provided. The eggs need to be incubated in vermiculite, and from start to finish hatching of the whole batch may vary between 160 and 360 days. It is always worth having a laying box with some vermiculite available for your female chameleons. Vermiculite is a herpetologist's favourite breeding medium as it is light, sterile and absorbs moisture readily. Sponge chips is another alternative used by some breeders.

Chameleons can climb extremely quickly when necessary, the long prehensile tail acting like a fifth limb. When they are hunting, their movements are slow and deliberate; when on the ground, they are much more cautious.

Uromastyx *Uromastyx acanthinurus*

Uromastyx, sometimes called Spiny Tailed Agamas, have a dry, parchment-like skin. Their colour varies from dull brown to sandy yellow or brick red. These inquisitive lizards make endearing pets with their tortoise-like head and postures. They are friendly creatures and can live for around 15 years.

must know

This tough-looking lizard thrives in the harsh, hot desert-like conditions found in the southern Mediterranean and Middle East and can grow to about 45cm (18in). During cold nights they wedge themselves between rocks.

Creating the right environment

Uromastyx are best kept individually – they are not a social species. Juveniles can be reared best in small plastic pet-home type units. Larger individuals and adults require vivaria large enough to run about in – 120 x 50 x 50cm (60 x 20 x 20in) is an adequate size for one lizard, but the larger the better, especially if you want to keep them in pairs or small groups.

Sturdy rocks with gravel or play sand make a good base. Provide a few retreats at the cooler end of the vivarium. In the wild, temperatures can reach over 45°C (118°F) and, to avoid overheating, Uromastyx retreat into cool burrows. Make them in a vivarium from drainpipes or cork logs but ensure that no heavy rocks or logs can collapse and injure your pet.

These lizards need the benefit of full spectrum light and hot basking areas, controlled by a thermostat. At the hottest point in the vivarium, temperatures should reach 35°C (95°F); the rest needs to be cooler at around 20–24°C (68–75°F). This is easier to achieve in larger vivaria. Night-time temperatures can also drop to 24°C (75°F). You can offer water a couple of times a week in shallow, accessible dishes. Mist spray occasionally, and a monthly bath or soak in a large dish is likely to be appreciated.

Handling

Uromastyx are not nervous creatures and, with patience, especially if you're starting out with a juvenile, your lizard will come to you for food. Slow movements are less likely to startle it, and eventually it should sit on your hand, at least for a while.

Feeding

Feed mainly green leaf foods with added pieces of vegetable and fruit. Food items should be finely chopped, especially for juveniles. Some insects may be accepted – up to three to five per cent of their diet. Feed every other day. Most of their water needs are met through food intake, so keep foods moist. Don't worry unduly if your pet rests without eating for one or two weeks. In the wild, this species aestivates at least for short periods, spending the summer or dry conditions in a dormant state.

Breeding

Mating occurs in spring and eggs should be incubated in dryish vermiculite at 30–33°C (86–89°F) for about 12 weeks. After mating, house the female on her own with a suitable amount of substrate to encourage egg laying.

must know

These lizards can wedge themselves into crevices and puff up their bellies to make it difficult for any predators to extract them. They have a special spiky club-like tail that can inflict serious wounds on their main predator, the venomous Horned Viper.

This delightful herbivorous lizard enjoys an occasional bath or spray with tepid water. The skin darkens and the body swells as life-giving water is absorbed. They grow to around 45cm (18in).

Savannah Monitor *Varanus exanthematicus*

Savannah Monitors are mostly found in grassland habitats across a wide area of Africa. They make excellent pets and can become extremely tame and placid – so 'laid back' that they have a tendency to slothfulness and obesity if overfed and under-exercised. Reaching a metre long, they should live at least 15 years in captivity.

must know

Australia is the true home of Monitors where the majority of species are found. Here they are called 'Goannas'. Monitors are members of the *Varanidae* family, which number around 40 species, including the world's largest lizard, *V. komodoensis*, or the Komodo dragon, at three metres (10 feet).

Behaviour of Monitors

These big, powerful reptiles are the juggernauts of the lizard world, capable of digging up river banks and termite mounds in search of food or shelter. As hunters, they are constantly on the look out for small animal prey and will climb trees, swim rivers and dig up other reptile eggs for a meal.

Creating the right environment

Savannah Monitors should be housed individually. A vivarium measuring 120 x 45 x 45cm (48 x 18 x 18in) would be adequate. Monitors require sturdy rocks, logs and heavy-duty water bowls. A cork or drainpipe shelter is essential in the cooler end of the vivarium. Movable furnishings, e.g. large pebbles, can offer temporary refuges for insects. This will encourage foraging activity as your Monitor moves the pebbles to get the tasty bugs. A simple set up is best, using a paper floor covering and a couple of main objects for basking on and hiding within. The daytime temperature gradient should range from 28–32°C (82–88°F), falling to 24°C (75°F) at night. Mist spraying bi-weekly should keep the humidity up at around 60 per cent. Bathing is much enjoyed by Monitors, and a weekly soak ensures your pet gets enough moisture and has the option of a long drink. Many lizards are stimulated to defecate in water, so water bowls must be cleaned regularly and fresh water given when fouling is noticed.

Handling

If purchased young, these Monitors should become very tame and suitable for occasional handling. They are usually placid, thriving in captivity and enjoying human companionship. I have never encountered aggression, although a bad Monitor bite would be painful and might require stitches.

Savannah Monitors are also sometimes known as Bosc Monitors. This young lizard may grow up to 1m (40in) in length.

These placid lizards have heavy 'armoured' scales and long sharp claws for digging and climbing.

Feeding

Monitors catch and consume their food whole. Young ones can be offered pink mice and larger insects. Adults eat whole adult mice and larger insect-type foods, e.g. locusts and snails. Feed two to three times a week as much as will be eaten in a three-to-five-minute period. Live insects scattered in the vivarium encourages foraging.

Breeding

Few people breed Monitors in captivity and you need a considerable amount of space. A female lizard would lay 20–50 eggs once a year. These are buried about 30cm (12in) deep and would need to be incubated for four to five months at around 29–32°C (84–88°F).

Water Dragon *Physignathus concincinus*

Water Dragons are an attractive lizard, with a long row of erect 'dragon'-like scales running along the back. Their overall colour is green, but the cheeks or jowls of the more mature males are enlarged and adorned with large pink scales. This makes these very placid creatures look quite formidable.

must know

Native to the steamy jungles of southeast Asia, Water Dragons are found in India, China and Thailand. They display well in the vivarium and reach 75-100cm (30-40in). They can probably live for 15 years and may be kept communally in larger enclosures with Basilisks or smaller Iguanids, as these species enjoy living in very similar conditions.

Creating the right environment

Larger vivaria suit these semi-arboreal lizards and a 90 x 90 x 60cm (36 x 36 x 24in) vivarium gives you room for all the essentials for optimum care. Although males are less aggressive to one another than other species, keep them alone or in the company of one or more females only. Juvenile Dragons, for the first year of life, can be kept in smaller units measuring, say, 90 x 30 x 45cm (36 x 12 x 18in).

These reptiles prefer semi-moist tropical conditions with a temperature range of 25–28°C (77–82°F), achievable with heat pads and spotlights, which may reduce at night to 20–22°C (68–72°F). Water Dragons like a large water dish and sturdy branches on which to climb and sun bathe (bask). Full spectrum lighting is also very important for its valuable UV benefits, helping lizards and plants to develop healthily. A substrate of chunky wood chips, logs and dense areas of real or plastic plants will help to create the right conditions for your pet.

Handling

Water Dragons are very suitable for occasional handling. They can remain static for long periods but are liable to shoot off every now and again.

Feeding

Water Dragons are primarily a carnivorous reptile. They will, however, eat a quantity of vegetative matter, possibly up to 10 per cent of their total diet. Adults feed greedily, and may consume mice, large insects, such as locusts and giant mealworm. Offer dandelion leaves, flowers and even canned 'fruit salad'. Feeding every other day when young and every two to three days as they mature is sufficient and ought to arrest the possibility of obesity, one of the greatest causes of sickness in pet animals. It is also advisable to supplement the diet of captive Dragons with a reptile multivitamin product.

Mist spraying is enjoyed and a large water dish should always be available. Dragons will bathe and drink from this, but are also likely to use it as a toilet, especially when you've just cleaned it out. Thorough regular cleaning is therefore essential. The water-soiling habit does eventually benefit the keeper as the substrate stays clean for long periods of time.

Magnificent Water Dragons love to climb, jump and splash around their vivarium. They will grow to around 70cm (28in) in length.

Breeding

Given space, a good environment and diet, Water Dragons are easy to breed. Females will lay up to 20 eggs, which should hatch around 70 days later at 28–30°C (82–88°F). These are usually incubated in vermiculite.

Plumed Basilisk *Basiliscus plumifrons*

Few lizards are as magnificently adorned as the basilisk, with its yellow eyes and bright green crests. Large males are armoured with a large crest on the head, along the back (dorsal crest) and on the tail. These are vibrant green, often marked with rows of blue spots.

The feet of all reptiles will suit the environment in which they live. Compare this basilisk's foot with one of a gecko, chameleon or monitor to see how differently they are adapted for their lifestyle.

Habitat

Plumed Basilisks are found only in Costa Rica, Panama and Nicaragua. Athletic sprinters they can run at speeds of 18mph over short distances and can take flight in an instant. They can even run across water – hence the name 'Jesus lizards' locally. Expect your pet to live around 10 years and grow to 75cm (30in).

Creating the right environment

Plumed Basilisks require spacious accommodation: a juvenile needs a 90 x 30 x 45cm (36 x 12 x 18in) vivarium, and most keepers will eventually make a custom-built unit about 2m (6ft 8in) long and 1.5m (5ft) tall or more to house adults. To thrive, males should always be housed individually or they will fight. Several females may be kept with a single male.

Basilisks enjoy daytime temperatures of 24–30°C (75–86°F), falling at night to 20–24°C (68–75°F). Humidity should about 70–85 per cent, so mist spray every other day. A large water bowl is essential as is a background of real or plastic plants with a sturdy branch beside or over the water. Other branches for climbing and basking on are appreciated, and basilisks will climb to quite a height to catch some rays or flying insects. Some shelter should be provided – cork logs are ideal as retreats.

Handling

If handled regularly, basilisks can become quite tame but are generally kept for their appearance. Never handle one outside; like many lizards, they can sit as still as a stone one second and then take off at great speed with no warning.

Feeding

Basilisks are fond of most medium and large insects. They benefit from eating small rodents (pink or fuzzy mice). Some plant material is also eaten and any foods considered suitable for omnivorous or herbivorous reptiles can be offered once or twice a week.

Breeding

Basilisks are easy to breed, provided you have the space to house a trio or more, i.e. one male housed alongside several females. Good nutrition will keep females in optimum condition as they may lay several clutches of 15–20 eggs per year. Eggs separately incubated in vermiculite take around 70 days to hatch. Juveniles need separating soon afterwards and require a well-supplemented diet.

must know

The basilisk's feet are remarkably adapted to enable them to avoid predators. They have delicate, enlarged flaps of scaled skin along the digits on the hind feet. On the downward movement of the foot upon water, these flaps open and, like a webbed foot, exert a greater resistance to the water. At great speed, without sinking, they can quite literally 'walk on water'.

This recently hatched captive-bred juvenile is ready for its new home. It still lacks the fine crest and colours it will develop as an adult.

Green Iguana *Iguanao iguana*

Iguanas are large tree-climbing lizards which graze on leaves, fruits and flowers in lush tropical habitats. They reach 160cm (64in) in length and can live for 10 to 15 years. They are generally green, but a huge variety of colours and patterns can be found in different populations within their range, and within sub-species.

must know

The family *Iguanidae* is a large one and virtually all the members are found in the tropical Americas and are egg layers. Among the iguana clan are the diminutive Anoles, the amazing looking American Horned Lizards and, of course, the Green and Rhinoceros Iguana.

Habitat

The Giant Green Iguana is native to tropical Central and South America where it prefers living in the vicinity of lakes, rivers or the sea. These lizards bask in the sun on branches that overhang the water, sometimes at quite considerable heights, and if disturbed they drop into the water below. Iguanas are good climbers, swimmers, divers and runners.

Creating the right environment

These truly magnificent reptiles are suitable only for pet owners who have the considerable space required to keep them as they grow. Iguanas need more space as they mature, height being the most important consideration. At the very minimum, a juvenile would require a vivarium measuring 92 x 38 x 38cm (37 x 15 x 15in), whereas an adult would need a custom-made unit of at least 120 x 180 x 120cm (48 x 72 x 48in). Increasingly, iguana owners use small rooms or walk-in vivaria, incorporating the sliding double glass doors that are available at home improvement stores. Iguanas should always be kept individually.

For substrate, use wood chips, leaf litter, pebbles or any similar material, including Reptile Grass – a

type of astro turf – and newspaper. Provide sturdy branches for climbing and basking on, and plastic plants for shade, plus a large non-spillable water bowl. Cork logs make good retreats. Delicate planting is not an option for this living dinosaur, which would quickly destroy real plants. A good hot basking spot

Iguanas are well equipped for an arboreal lifestyle. A long fourth finger and toe aid gripping and climbing. The muscular tail is an excellent tool for balance and helps propel diving or swimming Iguanas through the water.

Spur-thighed Tortoise *Testudo graeca*

These hardy creatures are native to the Mediterranean and are found in Spain, Greece and Turkey. They become very tame and recognize their keepers. More suitable for an enclosure than a vivarium, these tortoises require considerable space to thrive.

must know

Thousands of these tortoises are bred every year in captivity in the UK and USA. A captive-bred baby measuring 7.5cm (3in) is an ideal acquisition. Initially, it will need to be kept in a vivarium indoors in winter, and in an outside enclosure in summer. The shell colour can vary from yellow to black and they reach 20cm (8in) in shell length.

Creating the right environment

For all but the youngest juveniles, which need to be penned, tortoises may be kept in a walled or fenced garden for much of the spring and summer months when the garden is frost free. A hutch provides shelter from rain and excesses of temperature. It should be fitted with a heater pad or lamp to keep chills at bay and to enable the tortoise to be active on cooler days. Locate the hutch in a sheltered spot, away from direct wind and sunlight. Ensure that ponds and other deep water features are fenced off to prevent your tortoise drowning.

Despite its reputation, a healthy tortoise is a fast creature, which will crash through flowerbeds to smell plants before trying them. In the morning, tortoises like to orientate themselves towards the sun, and a south-facing slope is appreciated to help catch those all-important rays. They soon learn the location of their hutches, the best sun-bathing spots and favoured places to rest, feed or sleep.

Handling

Tortoises can be held firmly from either side, with your thumbs on top of the shell and your fingers underneath the body, but rarely is there a need to handle them. Tortoises tame quickly and will come to you, especially when they are offered tasty titbits. The tendency for their head to be withdrawn will gradually decrease as they become used to you.

Feeding

The Spur-thighed Tortoise is a herbivore and will be satisfied with most fruit and vegetable matter you offer. Vitamin/mineral supplements should be added to food to promote healthy shell formation, although access to some grazing in a garden and exposure to sunlight will usually fulfil most vitamin and mineral requirements.

Consider offering the following chopped foods, making sure you provide a good selection: beans, carrot, cress, peas, calabrese, lamb's lettuce, cauliflower, cucumber, sweet potato and soft fruits (not citrus). They can also forage – I positively encourage dandelions, a favourite tortoise food. Food preferences will vary, but experience will help

If kept under the right conditions, a captive-bred tortoise should live for at least 30 to 50 years.

to guide you. Lettuce should only be a small percentage of your tortoise's diet, no matter how much your pet enjoys it, since it is of low nutritional value. Although normally herbivorous, tortoises seem to enjoy a small amount of meat. Be careful not to overfeed on meat and restrict it to one to five per cent of their total diet.

Since tortoises hail from the world's naturally arid environments, most of the moisture they need comes from the foods they consume. However, during very hot, dry periods, additional water may be needed and tepid water can be dribbled or poured over your pet's head. They may then take the opportunity to drink a small amount. Alternatively, you may offer your pet tortoise some water in a shallow dish.

Breeding

The female has a shorter tail and a flat underside, while the male has a longer tail and a concave underside which enables him to mount the female for mating. The best male/female ratio for breeding tortoises is one male to three or four females. By ramming his shell against hers and biting, the male will force her to give up trying to escape and enable mating to take place. This rough courtship can cause considerable distress and injury to the female.

Eggs are buried about 15cm (6in) deep in the soil and are so well covered by the female that, unless egg laying is actually witnessed, it may be impossible to locate the site. The eggs must be removed, without turning, and placed in vermiculite at between 28°C (82°F) and 32°C

This captive bred juvenile is being held carefully using two hands. Tortoises need to be firmly supported when carried. It is best to transport them in a sturdy box.

(88°F) at a relative humidity of 70 per cent. Hopefully, the eggs will hatch approximately 75–85 days later.

For their first year of life, keep baby tortoises in an indoor vivarium under full-spectrum light at 25–28°C (77–82°F). Move them to small, contained runs in the garden during the warmest months, where access to real ultraviolet rays will help with healthy shell formation. At this stage, they are still vulnerable, so be aware of possible predators.

Hibernation

Hibernation is a natural feature of the European tortoise, and in temperate climates they need to be hibernated to avoid death from the extreme cold if kept outside. Some people bring their tortoises inside into large vivariums to allow them a rest period without actually cooling them or stopping them feeding, and this is an option. Hibernation is a natural process, however, and by gradually cooling your tortoise over a couple of weeks and stopping him eating, the digestive tract will be emptied. I hibernate mine in a ventilated box in loose dry compost covered in straw and placed in cool area with a stable temperature of around 3–7°C (37–45°F). Essentially, tortoises need gradual cooling, storing within a stable temperature range and checking regularly in case they are active. It is not recommended to hibernate baby tortoises until they have a plastron (shell) length of around 13cm (5in). Do some research if you haven't ever hibernated one before, because conditions vary from country to country.

want to know more?

• Thousands of books are available about reptiles in general and lizards and tortoises in particular. Look in your local library.
• A good web portal leading to articles, photographs and other websites on reptiles is www.kingsnake.com
• Wherever you live in the world you should be able to find local reptile or tortoise groups. Check your local library or community news for more information

4 Reptiles: snakes

Snakes are not only beautiful creatures but many are also remarkably friendly and easy to care for. Increasingly popular as pets, they are essentially low-maintenance animals that fit in well with modern lifestyles. Cheap to keep, with some adult supervision snakes are suitable for all age groups. Considerably less time-consuming than more conventional pets, most species make no noise, don't smell and cannot cause allergic reactions. As a good owner, it is your responsibility to ensure that the vivarium conditions are correct for your new pet to thrive. Your own preference and domestic situation should dictate what type of snake is most suited to you and your family.

What are snakes?

All snakes are reptiles and each and every one is a predator that consumes its prey whole. They are unable to chew or break their food into pieces, and this, in its way, makes the feeding of snakes for the pet keeper a relatively simple affair.

must know

Female snakes lay a leathery shelled egg. Most are simply laid in a depression or burrow, then covered and left. A few species, however, such as cobras and pythons, guard and protect their nests. Some species, mainly those from temperate areas, incubate their young inside their body and give birth to fully formed young.

Habitats

In the wild, snakes naturally inhabit a wide range of environments, from open sea to deserts, woodland and even tree tops. All snakes need to thermoregulate and rely entirely on their environment to satisfy their need for warmth. They may bask in the sun or coil up by a warm rock in order to heat up and become active. To avoid becoming too hot, they will also at times retreat into a den or burrow to cool down.

Physiology

Snakes have, in the distant past, evolved from lizards and are, in effect, specially modified limbless lizards. Periodic sloughing replaces their old skin, and it is always discarded, rather than consumed like many lizards and frogs. Their skeleton is elongated and consists of up to 400 separate vertebrae, mostly attached to long curved ribs. The usual vertebrate organs, including the heart, liver, stomach and lungs, are also elongated and protected by the extended rib cage.

Senses

Whilst snakes entirely lack an external ear and ear drum, they pick up airborne and earthborne sound vibrations along the body and through a small inner ear bone adjacent to the lower jaw. However, their main sensory organ is the forked tongue, which, flickering up and down and in and out, gathers tiny particles, pulls them back into the mouth. They are analysed by a structure in the roof of the mouth called the Jacobsons organ, which, in effect, smells and tastes the environment for the snake.

Scales

Snakes are covered in scales, which are hardened parts of the skin forming a protective outer covering and helping to prevent desiccation. Scales vary in size and shape, with larger, wide (ventral) scales found on the belly, and smaller ones along the body. Whilst different species have different numbers and arrangements of scales, an individual's scales may grow as it matures, but it will not gain nor lose the actual number of scales throughout its life. Snakes lack eye lids and cannot close their eyes, which are protected by a transparent (spectacle) scale.

The colouration of snakes is highly variable. Many have tones and patterns enabling them to blend in with their natural habitat. Others may use bright colours as a warning including this Milk Snake that is a mimic – pretending to be dangerous.

Californian Kingsnake

Lampropeltis getulus californiae

Thousands of beautifully patterned Kingsnakes are bred every year by hobbyists specifically for the pet trade. They are ideal pets in so far as they tend to enjoy handling, prefer small, secure caging and rarely suffer ailments or loss of appetite.

must know

Kingsnakes live in a range of habitats, from forests to deserts, and they may be found in the suburbs of some cities, in parks and gardens. They are an American species occurring over a large range from Canada in the north to Ecuador in the south.

Fierce predators

In their wild state, the Kingsnake is an aggressive and opportunistic predator, taking a large range of prey from lizards, birds and rodents, to other American snakes mentioned in this book. They are called Kingsnakes because they will actively catch, kill and consume even highly venomous snakes, making them, quite understandably, 'king of snakes' and a tolerated back yard snake in areas where dangerous snakes may also be found. Growing to about 1.2m (4ft) long, this medium-sized reptile should live for at least 10–15 years.

Subspecies

Several subspecies (closely related) exist and can be cared for in much the same way. Each has different patterns and colouration. Look out for the following:

- Florida King (*Lampropeltis getulus floridana*)
- Mexican Black King (*Lampropeltis getulus nigritus*)
- Speckled Kingsnake (*Lampropeltis getulus holbrooki*)

Whilst most Californian Kingsnakes appear banded with black and white hoops, striped forms are also available. As they are increasingly interbred in captivity, a wide variety of coloured and patterned forms are becoming available.

Creating the right environment

As Kingsnakes will eat other snakes (ophiophagos) they must be kept separately, even as juveniles, or you risk suddenly losing one of your pets. A clean dry vivarium measuring 90 x 30 x 30cm (36 x 12 x 12in) is more than adequate for an adult. A temperature gradient ranging from 24–30°C (75–86°F) is ideal.

Kingsnakes are not great climbers but it is worth giving them the option by providing a branch or two in the vivarium. Suggested furnishings would include a base substrate of paper, bark chips, leaf litter, or a mixture of the above. Water should always be available for them and regularly changed. Occasional mist spraying is beneficial, as would be the inclusion of a humidity box.

In the wild, Californian Kingsnakes are usually either banded, like the one above, or striped, where the black and white markings run along the length of the body. The darker markings range from jet black to a chocolate colour. The white markings are also variable: from creamy yellow to pure white.

Handling

The sooner you get to know each other the better for both of you. Kingsnakes should be at least part tame and definitely proven feeders before being

This glossy Mexican Black Kingsnake (*Lampropeltis getulus nigrities*) is in excellent overall condition; its scales are shiny and it is not too fat nor too thin.

purchased from a dealer. The very young are initially snappy and strike out, rapidly vibrating their tails as a threat defence posture – they have yet to learn that you mean no harm. However, Kingsnakes soon tame and will rarely offend their keeper by biting once they are conditioned to regular handling.

Feeding

Kingsnakes tend to feed well and the domestic mouse is all that they need as a diet for a healthy life. Most snakes are very hungry after a slough but they may refuse food just beforehand.

Without overfeeding them, allow a Kingsnake as much as it can eat in about 10 minutes every six to eight days on average. However, most snakes eat very regularly for some time, then, as they are 'fed up', they will refuse food for a while, particularly during a colder or winter/darker phase of the year.

Don't worry – this is perfectly normal snake behaviour. So much of our mammalian time is based on and around eating food that it takes some time for us to understand food from a reptile's perspective. This often consists of long periods with nothing to eat, followed by a sudden feast, but rarely any regular week-by-week feeding.

A multi-kill capacity

Unlike most snakes, which catch and constrict individual prey, the Kingsnakes have developed a multi-kill capacity and on finding a nest of rodents, for example, they can take one by the mouth but still hold and crush others within their coils and against the ground or burrow walls. This allows them to feast in times of plenty, so they can survive periods of scarce food availability. Of course, with pet snakes feeding on dead food, this phenomenon is rarely witnessed, but try offering your snake two dead mice at once and see what happens.

Breeding

These snakes are most likely to mate after a period of hibernation. They should be kept for several weeks, without any feeding, at temperatures of around 12–15°C (54–60°F). After this period, raise the temperature to their normal vivarium conditions (see page 121). When ready for mating, usually after a slough, the female releases hormones to attract the male. Mating snakes should be watched to ensure that one does not eat the other.

Return the female to her vivarium. Insert a laying container to provide a secure and comfortable spot in which to lay her eggs. About five to seven weeks after mating between five and seventeen eggs will be laid, each measuring up to 5cm (2in) long and 2cm (1in) wide. These should then be removed and incubated in vermiculite at 24°C (75°F).

Within 70 days, the eggs will hatch into 25cm (10in) long babies. Once sloughing has taken place, usually 12–16 days after birth, the young snakes will be ready to feed on the smallest of pinkies. At around four to six months of age, Californian Kingsnakes are an ideal purchase as a pet. This species of snake matures at two-and-a-half to three years.

> **watch out!**
>
> Most snake keepers will, at some time, usually by accident, get bitten. Apart from the initial shock, your snake is unlikely to cause itself or you much damage. Never put your hands close to a snake if you've been handling its food. You can't blame it for biting you if you wave around mouse-scented fingers. Antiseptic cream should be all that is required and a plaster for your bruised ego.

This chocolate and banana coloured Californian Kingsnake is one of the numerous colour morphs produced by breeders.

Sinloan Milk Snake
Lampropeltis triangulum sinaloae

Amongst the most beautiful of all pet reptiles, these bright, small snakes are widely available. Milk Snake is a term given to the smaller and more colourful members of the Kingsnake group. There are 25 recognized sub-species.

must know

Sinloan Milk Snakes have 'tri-coloured' bands of black, white and red along the length of their body. The red or orange bands are particularly wide in this pencil-slim Mexican species and they have a small black snout.

Habitat and behaviour

Milk Snakes inhabit the same types of habitat as Kingsnakes, but their range extends a little further north and south in the Americas. They range in size considerably, those in the north tending to be smaller than their relatives from warmer countries in South America. *Lampropeltis triangulum micropholis* from Costa Rica and parts of South America can grow to 1.5m (5ft). The Sinloan Milk Snake reaches up to 1m (40in) in length but is usually considerably smaller, averaging 60cm (24in).

Wild Milk Snakes are usually crepuscular/nocturnal creatures, but, in the security of the home they may be active at any time. However, they tend to spend much of their time secreted away in a hiding place. Wild Milk Snakes catch and eat small prey animals like lizards, rodents and even other Milk Snakes; for this reason, it is recommended that individual snakes are housed separately.

Creating the right environment

All Milk Snakes will require virtually identical care, with the larger species preferring more spacious accommodation. The small Sinloan Milk Snake is best kept in a small 60 x 30 x 30cm (24 x 12 x 12in) secure vivarium, which is warmed from below by a heater pad or cable to a temperature of around 30°C (86°F) at the warm end, giving the snake the option to move to the cooler end of the vivarium when required.

Milk and Kingsnakes are often fossorial (burrowing) and prefer deep substrate with no heavy objects, such as rocks, which may crush them as they hide or move amongst the substrate. Leaf litter, shredded aspen, bark and wood chips are ideal. Driftwoods, cactus skeleton and other lighter objects can be used to enhance the appearance of your pet's home.

These snakes do not like to be damp, and thus only a small water dish is required. A small humidity chamber can also be of benefit to assist shedding. A secure purpose-built vivarium is essential as these snakes are slight in build and great escapers.

Their stunning colouration makes Milk Snakes a popular first choice for novice keepers.

Named after the English naturalist H. W. Bates, Batesian mimicry is where an edible and otherwise unprotected species like the Milk Snake closely resembles a dangerous species – in this case, Coral Snakes. This evolution has occurred as a strategy to avoid predation, so the harmless Milk Snake falsely advertises itself as a dangerous animal rather than relying on camouflage and blending in with its habitat.

Handling

Most Milk Snakes become tame and easy to handle without any problems. When they are first handled, they can be a bit jerky in their movements but are fine for calmer hands. If you are unused to snake handling, sit down before you start – you would not want to accidentally drop a snake.

Snakes are less likely to tolerate handling during the first couple of days after feeding, and a nervous or scared snake may regurgitate food or even defecate on you. However, patience, persistence and common sense will help tame most snakes in a matter of weeks. Even if early on in your relationship, your snake does bite, it has such a tiny mouth that it can hardly do much harm.

Feeding

Rarely posing any feeding problems, Milk Snakes tend to prefer several smaller items rather than one very large one. Feed as often as any other Kingsnake, being very careful that no substrate is taken in alongside meals. By simply placing their food on a piece of paper substrate ingestion problems can easily be avoided. As with all snakes, feeding in separate containers is always advised (see page 122).

Your newly acquired Milk Snake should soon be settled into a diet of pinkies. Baby snakes will usually begin to feed after their first slough at about 10–14 days. They should then be offered two to three small pinkies at a sitting, once every five to six days. At several months of age (when they are best purchased as pets), they can be offered several pinkies or furries – as much as they will consume in about 10 minutes – every seven to ten days.

Once adult, feed your snake as much as can be eaten in 10–15 minutes, every six to eight days. The food a snake consumes should leave a visible, but not abnormal-sized, swelling along its body. You may find that after feeding well for a month or more your pet snake may refuse food for a number of weeks. However, do not worry if this happens – it is simply full and this is quite normal.

Breeding

These snakes are not sexually dimorphic, so there is no easy way for us to sex them. Most snakes will be sexed by the breeder or dealer who is supplying the specimen. For breeding information, see the section on Kingsnakes (see page 122), but, generally speaking, a cooling period or a 'brumation', as herpetologists now call it, is a good idea before any breeding is attempted. A typical clutch would be between five and eighteen eggs. If incubated in some vermiculite at 24°C (75°F), they should hatch around 60 days later.

Juvenile Milk Snakes are usually reared in small containers which will give them all their basic requirements, including heat, humidity and a sense of security.

Corn Snake *Eluphe guttata guttata*

Any attractive snake with a good temperament that feeds well and is easy to breed in captivity is likely to be very popular as a pet; such is the Corn Snake. These colourful snakes are native to the warmer parts of the United States, and are among the most sought-after species for first-time keepers and more experienced herpers.

must know

A medium-sized snake will measure between 80cm (32in) and 1.5m (5ft). They can breed from about two years of age and may live as a pet for 10-15 years, stopping breeding by about six years of age – their probable maximum natural wild lifespan.

Habitat and appearance

Corn Snakes are agile hunters, named after the corn fields and stores in which they search for rodent prey. Great climbers and burrowers, they can scale a tree trunk or root about under straw or hay with equal skill. With captive breeding, many colour 'phases' or morphs are routinely available, and juvenile Corn Snakes may be bought with names like Black Corn, Sun-kissed, Caramel or Zigzag, all referring to their colour or patterns. Its wild 'natural' colouration is blotched with burnt orange or red saddles, ringed in black over a tangerine background. The belly scales are frequently 'chequered' black and white.

Creating the right environment

Corn Snakes require a warm, dry vivarium with an average temperature range of 25–30°C (77–86°F), cooling slightly in winter to about 20°C (68°F). An adult pair should be provided with a 90 x 60 x 60cm (36 x 24 x 24in) vivarium. Newly hatched and juvenile individual snakes need smaller, more 'secure' units, such as a 25 x 10 x 10cm (10 x 4 x 4in) or a 60 x 30 x 30cm (24 x 12 x 12in) vivarium.

Any decorations should be thoroughly cleaned before placing in the vivarium, especially leaf litter,

which may introduce some unwanted pests into the snake's home. The overnight freezing of leaves will ensure that most potential pests, such as mites or ticks, are killed. The vivarium is simple to furnish as this snake is equally at home in woodland, pasture, a farm barn or a hole in a tree trunk. So logs, stones, cork logs, leaf litter, bark chips and climbing branches can all be used to decorate the vivarium for your viewing, and also to provide plenty of climbing areas as well as secure retreats for your pet.

Water, in a shallow dish, should be available at all times. As for most reptiles, this snake appreciates a periodic mist spraying almost as much as a 'humidity chamber'. As you gain experience of keeping snakes and learn to recognize how dry or humid a vivarium is and how to maintain a good balance between too little and too much humidity (air moisture), you can dispense with humidity chambers altogether. However, for many reptiles they are an invaluable aid to improving the quality of their lives and adding an element of comfort.

Corn Snakes will need access to fresh water for drinking and will really enjoy the occasional bath. Increased humidity helps snakes slough without difficulty.

Regular handling of juvenile snakes will condition them to human contact – they soon learn that contact will not harm them.

Handling

Corn Snakes rarely prove difficult to handle, but they are quite agile and can soon slip inside a sofa or under a floorboard. I find that these snakes prefer being approached from front-opening rather than top-opening vivaria. To a snake, there is something particularly threatening about sudden 'predatory' movements from above.

Baby snakes are usually very defensive to begin with and will hiss and strike out at anything that moves. Regular handling at this stage will condition or tame it to realize that humans mean no harm. Indeed, we are soon recognized as a good source of both warmth and food. Once it is being handled, the snake should calm down, and as it starts to feed

Attractive colourations and good temperament make these snakes a popular choice of pet.

over a few weeks it changes from a nervous baby snake to a more relaxed juvenile.

Feeding

Juveniles may be offered several pinkies or furries once every seven to ten days. Adults will require two to three adult mice every two weeks. About 60 small rodents will be needed in the first year of life, on average, making snakes surprisingly cheap to keep in comparison to some other pet animals. Be flexible with feeding – Corn Snakes' appetites will vary – but try to avoid over-indulging them as they will rarely refuse a feed.

Breeding

Breeding usually takes place during spring, and mating is characterized by an intertwined embrace. Mating in snakes provides an ideal opportunity to watch an ancient but effective reproductive process. A keen male will follow a prospective female around the vivarium, often biting her and rubbing against the length of her body. Eventually he will bite her firmly on the neck and put the weight of his body on top of hers. He will stimulate her by rubbing and making wave-like motions against her cloacal region and mating will take place. Courtship and mating can last for several hours.

Up to 20 eggs are laid in a concealed spot in the soil – suitable places are under a dish or log, or in a hide box. The eggs should be incubated in vermiculite at 28–30°C (82–86°F). They will hatch after around 10 weeks. Corn Snakes mature at two to three years, when they are about 80cm (32in) long, and can breed until they are about 10 years of age.

must know

Most male snakes have longer tails than the females. You can measure similarly aged snakes from the vent to the tail tip to ascertain the correct sex.

Yellow Rat Snake *Elaphe obsoleata quadrivittata*

The Yellow Rat Snake is a familiar and harmless snake which is regularly found close to human habitation in the eastern states of America in parts of Florida, Georgia, Carolina. A close relative of the Corn Snake, it is just as easy to keep in captivity and is widely available from captive-bred stocks.

must know

Laying many eggs is a survival strategy for reptiles. Snakes rarely offer any parental care of their young, which fend for themselves as soon as they are born or hatch from an egg. Having many babies, like the Yellow Rat Snake's 44 young, increases the chance that some will survive to adulthood.

Creating the right environment

A large snake, an adult is capable of reaching 2m (80in) or more, but it still prefers secure rather than spacious accommodation. A 120 x 90 x 45cm (48 x 36 x 18in) vivarium will suit a pair of snakes. With a temperature range of 25–30°C (77–86°F), they are frequently kept or bred by herpetologists in remarkably small and plain breeding units with paper as a substrate, a hide box and a water bowl.

This climbing (arboreal) snake enjoys some height and even elevated logs or a shelf to rest on and hide in. However, if you only have one or two snakes to look after, then you may prefer to establish a more naturalistic, attractive-looking vivarium. A large range of both natural and artificial materials are suitable to decorate it. As long as it is warm and can hide, the Rat Snake will remain unaffected by the simplicity or effort taken in decoration.

Handling

Initially very 'wild', baby Rat Snakes soon tame and are a popular snake for handling. Most snakes should not be handled for several days just after a feed. Some do not mind but others prefer to be left alone to allow the digestion of food in peace.

Feeding

Often referred to as chicken snakes in the United States, adult Rat Snakes will consume many prey items, including chicks and chicken eggs as well as mice, bats and other rodents or birds. Juveniles in the wild are more likely to take frogs and lizards. However, as pets they are happy to accept defrosted pinkies and mice. These greedy snakes are unlikely to ever become difficult to feed.

This impressive and potentially powerful reptile is highly variable in colouration, ranging through yellows to orange.

Breeding

Whilst many snakes are adversely affected by land development, farming, housing and forest clearance, Rat Snakes seem to thrive and their populations tend to increase when living alongside mankind. Saw mills, barns and log piles all offer ideal hunting territory, and compost or sawdust are utilized as egg-laying sites. Between five and 44 eggs are laid after mating in the American spring-time. Hatchlings, 30cm (12in) long, lack the distinctive stripes seen on adults. Their patchy pattern fades as they mature into adults over the first 12–16 months. The Latin *obsoletus* (worn out) refers to this gradual fading.

must know

This primarily diurnal snake is a true natural born killer and is of significant agricultural importance, capable of eating large numbers of 'pest' rodents.

House Snake *Lamprophis fuliginosus*

These slim chocolate brown snakes are a common African species and are frequently found in, under or near houses in villages and towns. In the wild, they feed mainly on rodents and lizards. Although not as common or as colourful as Corn and King Snakes, they are small and very easy to keep and breed.

must know

House Snakes are highly recommended for the novice keeper because they are rated as an easy-to-handle species and two or more can be kept together. They live for up to 15 years and can grow to 112cm (45in), although 60cm (24in) is more usual.

Creating the right environment

These snakes are best kept in a dry, woodland-style set up or just on plain paper. Shredded Aspen is great, but wood chips and leaves are much more decorative. Some suitable hiding places of natural material or shop-bought retreats are essential, as House Snakes just love hiding. A pair or, better still, a trio of one male and two females should be housed in a 90 x 45 x 38cm (36 x 18 x 15in) vivarium.

Water should always be available and a container with moist moss or sprayed plastic plants should be used as a humidity chamber. Provide a temperature range of around 25–28°C (77–82°F).

Secure and content within their shelter, juvenile House Snakes spend much of their time hiding.

Handling

Start to handle your snake as soon as you get it. House Snakes are, in my opinion, well suited to handling as a pet although, like many other species, they may bite or strike at sudden movements.

Feeding

These greedy snakes always seem to be hungry and are capable of taking quite large prey in relation to their head and neck size. In general, as a guide, hatchlings should be fed several small pinkies every three to four days; juveniles around two to three furries every six to eight days; and adults one to three adult mice every 10–14 days. However, some snakes will have smaller or larger appetites.

Breeding

Breeding is likely without adjusting the temperature or light cycles as is required in many other species. House Snakes breed from around a year old with the female laying 8–15 eggs per clutch. Incubate them at 27°C (80°F) for about 60 days, when the babies will hatch, measuring 20.5cm (8in). After a week, they shed and are ready to feed on small pinkies, at which point separate them to avoid fighting over food. Raise them in small secure tubs or pet homes until big enough to adapt to a larger vivarium.

Being a small species, House Snakes only require a moderate-sized vivarium and make a good introduction to snake keeping.

Royal Python *Python regius*

I recommend this attractive species as an excellent choice of pet snake, especially for beginners. Reaching a maximum length of 2m (6ft 8in), but usually smaller, Royal Pythons are never too large to become unmanageable and have a great temperament.

must know

In Africa, the Royal Python is often called the 'shame' snake due to its lack of fierceness. If disturbed or nervous, it curls up into a ball with its head buried under its coils, and hence its American name of Ball Python. This behaviour is rarely seen in captivity as it will adapt readily and happily to life as a pet.

Habitat

Native to West African grasslands and forest clearings, these snakes are solitary terrestrial creatures frequently inhabiting mammal burrows. Hunting mainly at night and during the early hours of morning and evening (crepuscular), they catch gerbil-like rodents for most of their diet.

Creating the right environment

You will need a vivarium measuring 120 x 45 x 45cm (48 x 18 x 18in) for keeping a pair of adults or several juvenile pythons. Initially, a baby python may prefer a much smaller 'pet home' – snakes often feel much more secure in small spaces, at least until they begin to grow and settle in. Several Royal Pythons can be kept together safely, but if kept alone they will not get 'lonely'.

Enjoying fresh air, a Royal Python's housing should always be well ventilated and heated within a 24–30°C (75–86°F) range. These snakes really enjoy their shelters and will frequently lie coiled within a cork log or similar bit of vivarium furnishing with just their head sticking out 'watching'.

A base substrate of newspaper is fine, but bark chips are much more attractive. Leaf litter also adds visual interest and enhances the appearance of

Never quite the same, like a fingerprint, every Royal Python has its own unique pattern to aid camouflage in the African bush.

most vivariums. As a terrestrial species, height is of little importance, but Royal Pythons will climb up and rest on top of cork logs or other shelters to bask or sunbathe. A spotlight or ceramic heater controlled by a thermostat is preferred, although in a warm house heater pads may be sufficient.

Most reptiles, including pythons, will enjoy an occasional bath. Mist spraying every so often is recommended, and a humidity chamber placed within their vivarium should help to prevent dehydration and ensure regular skin shedding.

Pythons are clean animals, going to the toilet only every 10–14 days or so, and hence cleaning is kept

Security is of paramount
importance to keep your
animals safe and secure.
Most herptiles can
squeeze through the
tiniest gaps. Exo-terra
and other modern
designer vivaria are
fitted with a door lock
and secure lid. Any cage
with glass sliding doors
should be fitted with a
lock or a rubber wedge.
Aquaria and vivaria
should be placed on a
polystyrene base. Use
electrical equipment in
accordance with the
instructions, and fit a
circuit breaker for safety.

to a minimum and soiled areas are easily removed.
Occasionally, snakes will toilet in their water bowl,
so this will need thorough cleaning before being
replaced with fresh water. It should be sited away
from any heat sources.

Handling

Royal Pythons are easy to handle, but do ensure, as
with all pets, that you support much of their body –
don't let them just dangle or jerk them around.
Most snakes wrap around you when being handled
– smaller ones on the hand, wrist and fingers; larger
ones on the arms and neck. Royal Pythons are too
small to cause any concern unless handled by a very
young child. If a Royal, or any snake for that matter,
is wrapping too tightly or won't let go, then reach
for its tail. Once you have a snake by its tail you are
effectively in control and can more easily unwrap
the animal than by tugging at the middle of its
body. These creatures are shy, cautious even, but
often very inquisitive when handled.

Feeding

A juvenile Royal Python should be offered foods
about once every six to twelve days, and adults
every 10–14 days. However, if well fed over a period
of time, these snakes are likely to refuse food, or
even 'fast' for a while, ranging from a couple of
weeks up to several months. However, there is no
need to be unduly alarmed at this: pythons lead
relatively inactive lives and have simply had enough
food. In time, particularly after the next 'slough',
feeding will resume. If in doubt about your python,
consult a herpetologist who will probably confirm

that it has had plenty to eat and otherwise in good health. Should you be concerned that your snake is actually sick, you should consult a herptile-familiar veterinarian. A record of its feeding habits would be a great help in any diagnosis.

Breeding

Large numbers of Royal Pythons are bred by hobbyists every year, and they are even available in a range of designer patterns and colouration. Adults are easily sexed by looking at their claws and tails from underneath. The tail and the claws are usually longer in males, with the twinned reproductive organ or hemipenis located below the vent, so a bulge is noticeable. Females can lay from three to fourteen eggs, but typically six to eight, which hatch some 60 days later.

This captive bred baby Royal is learning that its keeper poses no threat and will tame very quickly.

Woma or Sand Python *Aspidites ramsayi*

These docile pythons are found only in Australia, occurring across a range of habitats from the harsh, dry desert interior to more wooded coastal areas. They are prolific feeders and breeders and handle very easily, making them a popular and sensible choice of medium-sized pet snake.

must know

Unlike other pythons, the Woma and Black Headed Python lack the facial heat-sensitive pits that are used to detect prey. Some people speculate, probably correctly, that as they are both predominantly ophiophagus species, the heat pits that help other pythons detect warm-blooded prey may not have evolved in these ancient reptiles.

Appearance and habitat

Womas have small, dark eyes and a narrow head, which gives them a surprisingly un-python-like appearance. They vary in colour from a tawny olive brown through to a milky orange, pink and red. The body is heavily banded and the scales are both smooth and small. This is a very appealing snake, measuring an average 1.5m (5ft) in length. Some Womas can reach as much as 3m (10ft), depending on which part of Australia the original specimens came from.

Creating the right environment

For an individual adult snake, a 120 x 45 x 45cm (48 x 18 x 18in) vivarium is ideal. Juveniles prefer smaller accommodation, especially when you are establishing a new purchase. Womas are usually housed alone or, at the very least, they are separated when feeding – like the Black Headed Pythons, they are extremely ophiophagous (snake eating). Vivaria should be well ventilated, and front-access glass sliding doors are recommended. Most pythons are happy to be kept on paper, but shredded aspen, leaf litter and a host of other substrates can all be utilized to make a more

attractive enclosure. Shelters/hides are needed and a temperature gradient, using heating cable/pads or lamps, should offer the snake a 24-35°C (75-95°F) range. Water need only be offered on a weekly basis, and, as always, the occasional mist spraying is appreciated although humidity levels should be low. Womas, like many pythons, can expect a life span of 20-30 years in captivity.

Initially fetching very high prices, Womas are becoming more available and affordable as the captive breeding rates increase.

Handling

Womas are sensitive to sudden movements near the head, jerking back if your approach is too direct. Juveniles may be a bit jumpy at first but, like most pythons, soon tame with regular handling. Overall, this is a wonderful snake to keep and handle.

Feeding

This is a gorger of a snake, seemingly always eager to eat and very happy to consume mice or small rats. I suggest feeding all snakes outside their home vivarium after a short handling session and in a separate pet home container. This conditions the snake and reduces the chance of it striking hungrily at you when your hand goes in the cage to clean it or offer water. Offer an average two to three mice a week, but more or less depending on the size of your pet. With experience, you will get to know how hungry your snake is likely to be and how much to feed. Always separate Womas when feeding.

must know

Inhabiting frequently hostile and arid environments where drought is common, Womas can survive for long periods without either food or water, possibly for a period of up to 12 months or even more in their natural environment.

Unlike most other python species, the head of a Woma is more slender in appearance.

Breeding

Like all pythons, Womas are an egg-laying species and seem to breed quite prolifically. Breeding can be attempted at about two or three years of age. A seasonal or pre-pairing cooling is useful but not essential with this species. Overweight reptiles are less likely to breed successfully than healthy, well-nourished but trim individuals. Females will lay between five and twenty eggs per clutch but average around twelve. If allowed, they will remain coiled with the eggs until they hatch. The young should be separated as soon as they emerge from the egg, if not before. Young Womas are best reared in smaller containers initially.

When it is tightly coiled, the banded patterning of this West Australian Woma is clearly visible.

Children's Python *Liasis childreni*

Essentially a small and secretive snake, the Children's Python is native to most of Northern Australia but absent from the extreme south. This adaptable snake is as likely to be found in coastal forests as inland deserts, preferring to rest in termite mounds, under rock overhangs or other compact hiding places.

must know

A dark brown stripe behind the eye helps to camouflage this light brown, blotchy python. Underneath the wide belly, the ventral scales are usually a creamy white colour. Growing to a maximum of 1m (40in), this small and basically terrestrial species can live for up to 20 years.

Creating the right environment

An essentially warm and dry environment is key to successful husbandry. Temperatures of 23–30°C (74–86°F) are ideal, and, like many other pythons, a bad chill could be as life threatening as overheating. I recommend the use of both thermometers and thermostats to ensure that adequate but not excessive warmth is always maintained.

A 90 x 38 x 38cm (36 x 15 x 15in) vivarium is adequate, with a substrate of cork/wood chips. If a larger vivarium be offered, there must be secure, small hiding places available to provide the sense of security these snakes need. Most snakes prefer places they can squeeze into rather than a big cave.

Feeding

Wild Children's Pythons feed on any small mammal, bird, frog or lizard they are able to catch. Usually excellent feeders as pets, they take readily to their diet of mice or small rats. A few small mice offered every 10–16 days or so should be sufficient.

Handling

Never growing too large or becoming awkward to handle, these pythons have a good temperament.

Generally a very passive species, they are suitable for regular handling by their keepers.

Breeding

The silent male snake is attracted to a female by her 'smell' – a chemical, or pheromone, trail that she leaves for the male to follow. If you do attempt breeding, notice how excited a male snake becomes in the company of a female of the same species. The tongue flicks in and out more frequently, sometimes rapidly, at other times staying extended in long, slow and rhythmic movements. After stimulating the female by rubbing along the length of her body, the snakes entwine and mating occurs whilst they are paired. Contentedly mating snakes may be left together for a week or so before being separated, so a gravid female can develop in peace.

Between 10 and 50 eggs can be produced by these prolific pythons. Care for them in a similar way to most other pythons, keeping the incubating moss or vermiculite medium moist but not wet.

Growing to around a metre, small pythons, like the Children's, are easy to handle and may be more suitable as a pet for the beginner.

Black Headed Python
Aspidites melanocephalus

This spectacular-looking snake has an almost purple/black head and neck. Like the Woma, it is banded but more predominantly with creamy white or grey background scales.

must know

Black Headed Pythons are largely terrestrial but may live and hunt up on rocky outcrops or in rodent burrows. From a secure hole or ledge, they expose only their black head to absorb the radiant heat from the sun and thermoregulate effectively without revealing much of their body to potential prey or predators. Dark colours, such as black, absorb heat more effectively than lighter colours.

Habitat and behaviour

A muscular snake reaching up to 3m (10ft) but usually smaller, the Black Headed Python inhabits the northern third of the Australian continent over a vast range, living generally in more lush areas where prey is most numerous. It appears that both the Aspidities pythons share common traits. They multi-kill prey by squeezing several mammals at once and catch and eat large venomous snakes – reportedly not always asphyxiating them first but eating them alive – and are immune to the multiple bites from otherwise deadly snakes in the region.

Creating the right environment

A 120 x 45 x 45cm (48 x 18 x 18in) vivarium is ideal. Snakes should be kept separately and like a dry home with some opportunity to burrow in shredded paper, leaf litter or a similar substrate. Hiding spaces are appreciated across the heat gradient of the unit – 24-35°C (75-95°F) is a good range for this species.

Handling

Captive-reared specimens should pose no problems for handling. Initially they are often hissy but rarely bite. However, they may part-open their mouth and push your hand away when nervous. if you acquire

a young snake from captive stock, tame it quickly and accustom it to handling from an early age.

Feeding

Whilst captive specimens readily take mice or rats, wild Black Headed Pythons consume small lizards, monitors, mammals, birds and other snakes. Feed as much as they will eat over 10 minutes or so once every 12 days on average. Larger snakes will prefer rats to mice. They may go off their food if they are given a cooling option seasonally for a few months.

Breeding

The mating of entwined snakes can last for between 20 minutes and six to seven hours or more. Females produce five to ten eggs which hatch two to three months later. These should be incubated in some vermiculite, but some breeders let them stay with the parent coiled around them until they hatch.

Growing to around 3m (10ft), Black Headed Pythons are only really suitable for those keepers with a large vivarium.

A stunning and solid python, Black Heads are one of the more recently seen species available.

Carpet Python *Morelia spilotes variegata*

This very attractive medium-sized python is common throughout much of the Australian continent and New Guinea. It reaches a rare maximum length of 5m (16 ft 8in), although this is small in comparison to the longest snake in the world, the Reticulated python (*Python reticularis*) at 9-10m (30-33ft).

must know

The closely related sub species Diamond Python (*Morelia spilotes spilotes*) derives its name from its pattern of diamond-like marks and reaches 3m (10ft) on average, though specimens over 4.5m (15ft) have been reported.

Habitat and appearance

Carpet Pythons may be found in arid desert-like environments, living in burrows as well as high in the rainforest canopy, using their prehensile tail for extra climbing dexterity. In Australia, they are common around agricultural buildings, attracted by rodents or rabbits. Their markings vary considerably, from a black and grey with blotches and stripes to a high yellow or rusty colour. The name apparently comes from the 'oriental carpet' look of the patterns.

Creating the right environment

These snakes need a large dry vivarium at 23-30°C (74-86°F) with ground and elevated shelters. The base should be covered in paper or wood chips.

Good climbing branches need to be sited at a safe distance from any light bulbs or ceramic heaters. A heater pad or two on the floor should keep even the largest cages warm but must be carefully monitored with a thermostat. As they mature, snakes should be housed in larger cages or enclosures – around 180 x 60 x 60cm (72 x 24 x 24in) is adequate for medium-sized specimen. Good ventilation is always important but draughts must be avoided.

Handling

Carpet Pythons are quite good for handling, but large snakes are never as relaxing to hold as smaller ones. Few big snakes ever settle down on your arm or in your pocket. They tend to reach about or coil too tightly around whatever else is nearby and are less likely to settle down calmly. Many snake keepers enjoy large snakes for the sheer pleasure of watching their behaviour and natural beauty.

Feeding

A popular pet species, this impressive snake will eat any bird or mammal offered. My own specimen, a 3.5m (11ft 8in) male, is captive-bred and a good defrost feeder. He is rarely handled, only every month or so, especially when the vivarium is soiled or needs a good clean out. He is very tame and has progressed to rats now that he is too big to bother with mice. Feed according to size and every week or so. The amount eaten will vary according to size and appetite, Like many species of snake, some will bathe regularly and others never or seldom. Always offer Carpet Pythons a water bowl, preferably quite a large one, but they may rarely use it.

must know

Capable of laying between 10 and 50 eggs, but usually around 20, these are deposited in a typical python mound that the mother will, if allowed, coil around until they hatch 10–15 weeks later. Most breeders remove the mother and incubate the eggs separately with vermiculite or sphagnum moss.

Carpet Pythons are suited to keepers able to provide spacious accommodation and need to be well supported when handled.

Common Garter Snake
Thamnophis sirtalis sirtalis

Native to the United States from the Atlantic to the Pacific, these snakes are small, slim and active. Beautifully marked with creamy lines and reddish flanks, they hunt in largely aquatic environments and will catch and eat both fish and amphibians.

must know

Garter Snakes rely greatly on sight for hunting. As a diurnal predator, they can track by both sight and scent, seizing their prey firmly in the mouth. Prey is generally too small and defenceless to require constriction and most foods are swallowed alive, head first.

Creating the right environment

Over 50 types of Garter Snake exist and can all be kept under similar conditions. An adult pair prefer a 120 x 38 x 38cm (48 x 15 x 15in) vivarium or larger. Juveniles should be reared in smaller containers. You need a dry vivarium equipped with a good-sized water bowl and substrates, such as wood chips and leaf litter. Logs, branches and even living ferns may be incorporated, offering spaces to explore and hiding places. A humidity chamber is essential for good skin conditioning. Keep the substrate warm with a heater pad, with a temperature range of 20-26°C (68-79°F). If using spot lamps for overhead heating, they should be controlled by a thermostat.

Handling

These snakes generally handle well – only very nervous individuals may defecate on you but this is rare and usually only happens whilst a juvenile or wild-caught snake is going through the first steps of taming.

Feeding

Large water bowls are preferred, and many keepers remove their snakes to another container at feeding time. They should be fed separately if several snakes live together, as they have a tendency to fight over food. When two snakes get hold of the same item, one may end up eating the prey as well as the other snake. Garters enjoy exercising in a shallow bath, and if fed outside their main vivarium are likely to feed, then defecate, considerably easing your cleaning routine. Having defrosted your fish, it may be that simply placing it in a shallow water dish is sufficient to get your snake interested. Initially, it is often best to 'wriggle' the food about a bit on long tweezers. Once the snake recognizes this as 'live' food, it will soon learn to accept the same type of food in future from a bowl. Small rodents, pinkies and earthworms are also likely to be taken by many Garter Snakes.

Breeding

Garter Snakes are live-bearers and the young grow rapidly if fed correctly, maturing at eight to ten months. The number of young can vary between subspecies and depends on the age, experience and health of the female; between 10 and 80 young per litter is typical. Sperm is retained by females and they may produce young up to two years after one mating.

The keeled scales, each with a ridge, make the enchanting Garter Snake rougher to the touch than many other species.

Rough Green Snake

This gentle, small, grass green, diurnal insect-eating snake is usually found in the vicinity of streams, meadows and marshes. It is native to the eastern United States from New Jersey to Florida and westwards to Texas, Kansas and into northern Mexico.

must know

All snakes have scales, made from a hard substance called keratin, which is also the basis of hair and feathers. Every species has a different pattern and many have some larger scales called shields. Rough Green snakes have rough or keeled scales, i.e. with a ridge in the centre. They help give a better grip and can be rubbed together to make a threatening noise.

Creating the right environment

Green Snakes can be kept in groups or on their own, and may share a community vivarium with other similar-sized non-cannibalistic species, such as Garter Snakes. They enjoy temperatures in the range of 24–28°C (75–82°F), established with the combination of a heater pad and spotlight controlled by a thermostat. They are best housed in a dry but regularly mist-sprayed vivarium; they won't like it too damp but will thrive with slight humidity. By decorating their vivarium of at least 90 x 38 x 38cm (36 x 15 x 15in) with some mosses, a greater depth of leaf litter and incorporating a humidity chamber, you will not go far wrong. A lightweight snake, fine branches or house plants will give them something suitable to climb on. Their lifespan is around 10 years.

Delicate and beautiful, Green Snakes are a social species that may be kept in groups.

Handling

As their name suggests, these snakes have rough or keeled scales and they do not slide through the fingers like so many smooth-scaled snakes. They are, however, simple to handle albeit delicate.

Feeding

One of the things people like most about Rough Green Snakes is that they do not need to be fed rodents but are happy to exist on a diet of insects, such as crickets, spiders and the occasional small vertebrate. In the wild, they occasionally consume small lizards and frogs, so I advise a varied diet where possible, even offering the occasional nutritious pinkie. They are unlikely to eat dead foods, but are fascinating to watch stalking a big, fat juicy cricket, grasshopper or millipede. Feed on a regular basis, say, every other day – but avoid meal worms as these are less palatable and less nutritious than crickets and other available live foods.

Breeding

Due to the fact that this is a 'common' snake, little effort has been made to captive breed them on a regular basis, although use of pesticides is severely affecting some populations. They are quite legally collected and exported under a monitoring system, so do not be concerned about keeping a wild-born snake. Perhaps eventually you will become a Rough Green Snake specialist and breeder. An average of two to six eggs are laid at a time.

Take care when handling Rough Green Snakes as they are quite delicate.

must know

Rough Green Snakes can reach about 90cm (36in) in length. Semi-arboreal, they have superb camouflage which effectively makes them disappear whilst climbing low vegetation.

Bull Snake *Pituophis elanoleucus sayi*

Bull Snakes are large and powerful predators that feed almost exclusively on small mammals. Variable in their patterning and colouration, they are one of America's most attractive snakes.

must know

Surprisingly, most snakes are silent and unable to hiss. The Bull Snake has a special membrane or skin flap in its windpipe and this, being vibrated by exhaled air, makes a loud hissing/rasping type sound. The name Bull Snake comes from the sound that large specimens can make, reminiscent of a 'bull' snorting and grunting.

Habitat and behaviour

Fifteen subspecies are known, ranging northwards just into Canada right down into Central America. Bull Snakes are popular with cereal-growing farmers and are apparently still caught and even purchased for release into barns where they eat rats, mice and squirrels. They are noted for the noises they make and their violent defence posturing. An irritated or threatened snake inhales a considerable quantity of air, swelling itself to appear larger than it really is. With its open mouth and a typically serpentine 'S'-shaped body posture striking up towards its real or imagined foe, it makes for quite a scary encounter. However, like most snakes, even venomous ones, it is largely bluff and the snake would really prefer a hasty retreat than a violent confrontation.

Creating the right environment

A large vivarium, 150 x 60 x 60cm (60 x 24 x 24in) is ideal for an adult or breeding pair of these secretive but quite active snakes. They need a warm and dry vivarium with height as they will climb, but they also enjoy burrowing under the paper or wood chips at ground level. Finer substrates like sand can irritate their skin, so chunkier moss, bark chips or just plain paper are best. A temperature range of 24–28°C (75–82°F) is adequate, and an under-floor heat pad warming the substrate, is recommended. Use a spot lamp to create a basking area, which must be controlled by a thermostat to avoid overheating.

Water should be available at all times although this snake does not enjoy bathing. Occasional mist spraying will help as it is most at home in a semi-arid desert or dry-forest type of habitat.

The wide ventral (belly) scales are visible underneath this Bull Snake. They give snakes a good grip on a variety of surfaces and aid movement.

Handling

Juvenile captive-bred specimens are best as they are already adapted to handling and life in a vivarium. As they grow, the power and potential size of these snakes becomes apparent. Although they can reach over 2.1m (7ft), 1.5m (5ft) is more average, but they are quite a handful at only 60cm (24in). They are safe to handle although strong and persistent, but not suitable for unsupervised handling by a child.

Feeding

Bull Snakes are unlikely to refuse any suitably sized mammalian or bird prey; all rodents are accepted. In the wild, these may be dug out of their burrows with a combination of the body loops helping to shift soil and an unusual raised scale situated on the tip of the snout. Feed every seven days on average.

Beautifully patterned Bull Snakes are somewhat secretive but they feed well and are now a popular choice for the herpetologist.

Brazilian Rainbow Boa
Epicrates cenchria cenchria

Rainbow Boas are common in many regions of South America, including Brazil, Guyana and much of the vast Amazon basin. This naturally nocturnal species inhabits a wide range of conditions, from rainforest to grassy plains and scrub land.

must know

The underlying colour of these snakes is basically a reddish-brown hue with rings and spots along the entire length of the body. A variable species for shades of colour, the spots and rings tend to fade as the snakes mature into an average length of 120cm (60in), but potentially growing to 190cm (76in).

Iridescent scales

Their name is derived from their iridescent scales, which, like oil on water, display a vivid spectrum of shimmering colours that change according to the light and angle of vision. Rainbow Boa scales have microscopic ridges that act like a prism – refracting sunlight into a stunning show of colours. It probably aids in defence and makes it hard for a predator to pinpoint the exact location of the snake.

Creating the right environment

These snakes are simple to keep and easily tamed. They need a warm, dry vivarium with a temperature range of 22–30°C (72–86°F) with some humidity, but never damp. A 90 x 38 x 38cm (36 x 15 x 15in) vivarium should be fine for most snakes, or a 120 x 38 x 38cm (48 x 15 x 15in) one for a larger specimen. An occasional mist spray is sufficient to keep the atmosphere fresh and just right.

Feeding

These are lazy snakes, preferring to wait and ambush their meals rather than giving chase. Like all boas, they are naturally inclined to feed on birds and mammals, the dexterous long jaws opening to consume surprisingly large prey items. The heat-sensitive pits, situated on the mouth, give the snake's brain a thermal image of its warm-blooded prey; thus it may help if you warm up the food you offer to your snake, so it has a better image of its meal.

Most are kept, grown and even bred on an exclusively rodent diet. Take care not to overfeed – avoid obesity in all pets. You should soon notice when a good feeder simply becomes an overeater.

Breeding

Like all boas, these snakes give birth to living young and are a relatively easy species to attempt breeding from, should your interest for them grow. A short cooling-off or brumation period is advised before attempting to pair adults. If successful, mating behaviour should be seen almost immediately. They can be kept communally but are usually and satisfactorily housed in separate vivariums.

With shimmering body scales, these South American reptiles are a highly desirable pet snake.

Boa Constrictor *Boa constrictor*

Boas are the largest snakes that are most frequently kept and bred in captivity. For decades, they have been a popular pet in the Americas, as their geographic range begins in Mexico and extends southwards through Central America down into South America.

Appearance

Boas seem to improve in colouration as you travel south through their range. Amongst the most desirable of Boa Constrictors are those with red tails – the Red-tailed Boas (*Boa constrictor ortonii*) are native to Peru and are very attractive with deep blood-red colours along the lower back and tail.

Boas are beautiful snakes with an unusual texture to the touch, which is more fabric-like than scaly. They have a basic creamy, silver colouration with diamond-shaped patterns and a peppering of spots. The colouration of Boas is variable amongst the 11 recognized, closely-related sub-species, but they are all normally very attractive.

Heavy-bodied, Boa Constrictors can range from 2–4m (6ft 8in–13ft 4in), but 3m (10ft) specimens are a more common adult size. They are good climbers, feeding on mammals and birds in the wild.

Creating the right environment

Ensure that you really are capable of caring for and housing any snake before you purchase one of these. As a Boa Constrictor grows, it will require larger food items and eventually a big vivarium. A spacious, dry vivarium needs to be warmed within a 25–32°C (77–88°F) range to provide comfort for a

Boa Constrictor. Only sturdy climbing shelves or branches are suitable for such a chunky snake. Cork logs are ideal for offering a sense of security, but Boas are quite happy to be in full view most of the time. Zoological gardens have long preferred them for show as, unlike many snakes, they may be on 'display' for long periods. Any substrate will suit this species, but avoid sand and the finer grades of wood or bark chips. A large water bowl is welcomed and your Boa will bathe occasionally, often for many hours or days at a time. Mist spray occasionally to freshen up the environment.

Handling

Boa Constrictors are large snakes and should be handled with care. With long teeth and a powerful bite, Boas are best kept and handled under adult

must know

People get confused by Boa Constrictors and 'bone constricting'. Boas grasp their prey, preferably on the head, and squeeze it. The prey is stunned by the initial strike, unconscious and dying within seconds from asphyxiation, not from 'crushed bones'. As predators go, snakes are quick and humane at dispatching prey.

Cryptic colouration helps the Boa Constrictor blend in effectively with its natural environment.

You need plenty of space to successfully house a snake as large as a boa in captivity.

supervision, even though most pet ones, which are well tamed and cared for, will never bite. Larger specimens may need two or more people to help lift them and maintain control. Tame specimens pose few problems, but an aggressive large Boa requires careful and firm handling. A bite would hurt and require medical attention. To transport a snake, all but the smallest are usually placed in a cloth bag, pillow or duvet case, tied securely at the top. Smaller specimens can be transported in their pet homes.

Feeding

Like all the larger snakes, Boas are best fed with caution. Prey should be dropped onto the floor or wiggled on long tweezers for younger specimens that have not yet adjusted to taking static rather than 'living' food. Boas will accept mice, rats or small rabbits as well as the occasional chick and young chicken. With a large, greatly expanding jaw and neck, they easily consume prey items much larger than you might imagine possible – until, that is, you get to know snakes better.

Smaller prey

Smaller prey offered in greater quantities may be more efficient if you wish to handle your snake regularly, as the smaller items are more quickly digested, making handling less uncomfortable for the Boa. One of the main benefits of having a defrost feeding regime is that snakes are tamer and thus less likely to be alert to any movement representing a possible food source. They become conditioned to expecting dead static items to eat and are less likely to bite or strike out.

Boa Constrictors have an unusual mottled belly, or ventral scales.

Breeding

Boa Constrictors are relatively easy to breed and they can be seen copulating many times over a few weeks if they are successfully paired. The young develop inside the mother who will bask more often to keep her developing babies warm. The 30–60 live young, measuring around 48cm (19in) or so, will feed after their first skin shed and are completely independent from birth.

Waiting for food this boa is barely visible on the forest floor.

want to know more?

- For numerous articles, photographs and other websites, log on to www.kingsnake.com
- Do some research to find a herpetological society local to you. Look on the Internet or ask in local pet stores
- Books are available on the natural history or care of snakes. One of my favourites is *Living Snakes of the World* by John M. Mehrtens (Sterling 1987). Check out your local library, book shop, pet store or the Internet.

5 Invertebrates

Some invertebrates are very attractive and can make fascinating pets. In fact, they are the most diverse creatures on our planet, and we share our world with literally millions of species which number many billions of individuals. Several types are ideal for children to manage alone, requiring a minimal amount of cleaning or specialist equipment to maintain. They frequently have a short natural lifespan and will never require veterinarian treatments or grooming. A vivarium can house many invertebrates, which, with their interesting life cycles and behaviour, make surprisingly absorbing and educational pets.

What are invertebrates?

The majority of living creatures on earth are invertebrates, and a single swarm of locusts can contain more individuals than the whole human population. Invertebrates include all the animals without backbones, such as the squid and clam, as well as the more familiar creepy-crawlies, like insects, worms and spiders.

must know

Many invertebrates have a special body structure called an exoskeleton, which is a hard external shell as seen on a millipede or Praying Mantis. Other species, such as worms, are composed entirely of soft tissues.

Ectotherms

All invertebrates are ectotherms, which means they are reliant on external sources of heat to maintain their bodily functions. Interestingly, some species have been found to survive in extreme conditions, both above and below what scientists conventionally term fatal temperatures – for example, under ice caps and at volcanic thermal vents.

Feeding and diet

Invertebrates consume a variety of foods; some, such as Praying Mantids and spiders, are carnivores, while others, such as Stick Insects and Leaf Insects, are herbivores. Cockroaches, however, are scavengers, willing to consume almost anything on offer. Depending on the species, foods may be grazed, hunted, ambushed, trapped, snared or even lured.

Handling

In general, inverts are the least handleable of all the animals featured in this book. If in doubt, don't handle them. They should not be moved or handled during a moult, when they are very vulnerable to damage. Soon after a moult, an invertebrate's body hardens and they can then be handled if necessary.

Adult supervision is essential when young pet keepers wish to move or handle these creatures. Only a few species are suitable to keep as household pets.

Arthropods

All the invertebrates in this book are classified as Arthropods, i.e. animals with an external skeleton and jointed limbs. Arthropods have to regularly shed their external skeleton or exoskeleton as they grow. Most belong to several major groups, as listed below.

Insects

All have three pairs of legs and three parts to the body – the head, thorax and abdomen. Stick Insects, Leaf Insects and Praying Mantids are all insects.

Millipedes

Millipedes have many body segments and elongated bodies. Each body segment has two pairs of legs. Their close relative, the Centipede, has a single pair of legs per body segment and is a venomous predator, whereas Millipedes are herbivores.

Crustaceans

Crustaceans are characterized as being mainly aquatic hard-shelled creatures, but the Hermit Crab is land based although it still breathes through gills.

Arachnids

Spiders and Scorpions, along with Harvestmen, ticks and mites are types of arachnids. They have eight jointed legs and, frequently, two main body parts – the cephalothorax and abdomen.

must know

Invertebrates have essential roles in most ecosystems: they not only eat and recycle rotting vegetation but they inhabit the inside and outside of most other living creatures. They may be found living on all continents, from high peaks to deep underground and in both fresh and saltwater environments.

Invertebrates are found in seemingly endless variety. Whilst many lack legs, wings and even an exoskeleton, this Praying Mantis is a classic insect.

Indian Stick Insect *Carausius morosus*

Indian Stick Insects are one of the easiest of all the invertebrates to manage. A classic classroom pet, they are a good introduction to keeping and learning about creepy-crawlies. Their bodies are long and 'stick'-like, growing to 11cm (4in) and living for a year.

must know

Care must be taken if keeping cut plants in jars of water as the Stick Insects will fall in and drown. Try to find narrow-necked jars or pierce holes in the lids of water-filled tubs.

Each tiny egg is like a small jar. The baby Stick Insect must prize open the lid to emerge.

Appearance and behaviour

Stick Insects are usually green or brown with bright red markings on the inside of their forelegs which are flashed as a warning when they are disturbed. If threatened, they often drop to the ground and remain motionless like a twig. When the threat has passed, they stretch out their legs and start moving again, gently swaying like a twig in the breeze.

Creating the right environment

These insects require a tall vivarium measuring at least 30 x 45 x 30cm (12 x 18 x 12in), as they live mainly on food plants. Keep them warm at around 24°C (75°F). However, they are a tolerant species and are happy at room temperature, although they do dislike temperature extremes.

Humidity levels

A reasonable level of humidity is required, so mist spray but do not let them get soggy or mouldy. A thirsty Stick Insect exercises its mouth parts continuously and a quick spray of droplets onto a leaf soon quenches its thirst. Paper is quite good for lining the floor of the vivarium as it is easy to remove for cleaning, but damp peat, leaves or moss may look nicer and increase humidity levels.

Handling

These creatures tame easily but need careful handling. Gently pick up your insect between finger and thumb, or offer your flat palm and tap the creature gently so that it walks onto your hand. Legs that get stuck or hooked onto an object or piece of clothing need a gentle nudge to loosen their grip.

Feeding

Herbivorous by nature, Stick Insects eat only plant matter throughout their entire lives. Most are reared on privet or bramble (blackberry) leaves and will prefer tender new leaves on young plants. These should be potted up and changed regularly to ensure an abundant supply. Freshly cut sprigs of privet or leafy lengths of bramble can be used, but un-potted stems need replacing frequently.

Breeding

Stick Insects are capable of reproducing without mating. An adult female lays fertilized eggs, measuring 2–3mm ($^1/_8$in). Hundreds of tiny eggs are laid during her lifetime, several a day during the peak of fertility. Hatch the eggs on vermiculite or sand, keeping them warm and spraying occasionally. Check them periodically. They can take up to a year to hatch. The young require the same conditions as adults but keep them with similar-sized individuals. They will moult (shed their skin) six times before reaching adulthood, only a few months later.

Indian Stick Insects not only live on but also eat plants such as Privet, a commonly available and fast-growing plant.

Leaf Insect *Phyllium sp.*

These incredible little creatures look just like the leaves they feed on. Green and flat, they even develop brown spots and tatty edges to affect superb camouflage. They are native to warm, humid rainforests in Asia – Malaysia and Thailand – as well as New Guinea, Australia, Madagascar and the Seychelles.

must know

Depending on the species available, the adults measure 8-15cm (3-6in). Leaf Insects are shorter lived and more difficult to maintain and breed than Stick Insects, but are well worth the additional effort.

This juvenile Leaf Insect, seen alongside a pencil for scale, is one of the many remarkable insects that may be kept in a large group.

Creating the right environment

A 60 x 45 x 30cm (24 x 18 x 12in) vivarium will house up to six individuals. Whilst preferring temperatures of 21-27°C (70-80°F), they do not like stagnant air, so good ventilation is essential for optimum growth and development, especially during a moult. Maintain the temperature with heat pads or keep in the warmest part of the house.

Since Leaf Insects are arboreal, choice of substrate is largely decorative. However, plain paper should be placed on the base of the vivarium when they are breeding, so eggs may be located easily. Wood chips or even moss, kept moist, help to keep humidity at around 70 per cent. Regular mist spraying with tepid water and a hygrometer are recommended, but after a while you will get to know when they are satisfied with your efforts to create a home for them.

Handling

Adults may be encouraged to walk on to your hand. They wobble about in a comical fashion, trying to convince you that they are a leaf blowing in the breeze. Handle them with care because it is so easy to damage these very delicate creatures.

Feeding

In captivity, Leaf Insects live and feed on bramble leaves. Old cut sprigs need replacing every other day, or, ideally, small plants can be potted up and placed directly in the vivarium, then rotated to ensure that fresh growths are available. You can also try them on oak, guava and rambutan leaves.

Breeding

These small invertebrates have a life expectancy measured in months, not years, and at about four months of age they are ready to breed. Males have slimmer bodies, longer wings and antennae. One hundred or more eggs are produced and drop to the ground. These, amazingly, are also camouflaged and look like the droppings of caterpillars. The parents die not long after they have finished laying eggs. By keeping the eggs warm, the young will emerge anything from a few months to over a year later. Tiny bright red (ant-like) babies will climb onto plants and start feeding immediately. If you are successful with these insects, you can maintain a constant life cycle with eggs, growing babies and adults laying at the same time.

A spectacular natural mimic relying entirely on camouflage for its defence, the Leaf Insect is unable to defend itself in any way except its leaf-like disguise.

Giant Millipede *Epibolus sp.*

In Africa, these creatures are called 'jungle trains' or 'chongaloloo'. Of the 10,000 types of millipede known, only a few are regularly kept as pets, and amongst them is the Giant Millipede, which is essentially an animal of the soil and leaf litter.

Appearance and behaviour

Giant Millipedes are easy to establish and breed if several are kept together as a colony. They may be reddish-brown or black, and some species are even striped. Growing to 25cm (10in), they can live for several years if they are kept in the right conditions. Millipedes are slow, harmless terrestrial scavengers and should not be confused with centipedes.

Creating the right environment

You need a large and wide, rather than high, container. One measuring 90 x 45 x 30cm (36 x 18 x 12in) or 60 x 30 x 30cm (24 x 12 x 12in) is a suitable home. Add chemical/fertilizer-free compost to a depth of 8–10cm (3–4in) and cover with leaf litter. Maintain a temperature of 24–27°C (75–80°F) using heat pads. Keep the vivarium humid and balanced somewhere between dry and damp. A set up like this will only need cleaning out completely once or twice a year, providing great compost from digested leaf litter.

Feeding

Oak, sycamore and vine leaves, amongst others, and various mosses are ideal. I advise pre-freezing leaves in bags in order to avoid introducing other invertebrates into your set up. Besides eating leaf

This tamed Millipede is crawling on its keeper's hand. If disturbed, it would rapidly curl up into a defensive coil.

litter, small pieces of fruit
and vegetables can also be
offered on shallow dishes
or upturned lids, so they are
easy to remove before spoiling.
Leaf litter should be added liberally to a
depth of several centimetres and topped up as it
gets consumed. Millipedes will drink from mist
sprayed droplets or very shallow tub lids or dishes.

Handling

If you are gentle, Millipedes tame quickly, and it's an
amazing feeling to have one on your hand. Their legs
move in ripples like a Mexican wave. They are active
at night or under crepuscular (low light) conditions.
Many species can secrete unpleasant fluids from
glands along the sides of the body when disturbed
or irritated – these may smell, sting or stain hands
and clothing. They also curl when disturbed, whilst
sleeping or during a moult, when they remain
inactive for a while and should not be disturbed.

Each body segment is supported
by two pairs of legs, and every leg
has tiny hooks which enable the
Millipede to travel quickly along
the ground.

Breeding

Males are easily sexed if viewed from underneath –
gonopods are visible on the seventh or eighth segment.
These are modified legs for transferring sperm to the
females. In males, they are frequently hidden from
view – you may just see a stump. Millipedes wrap
around each other to mate, and some then build
a nest in which to lay eggs. Should yours breed,
you would soon notice numerous babies crawling
around the leaf litter. Initially, these have far fewer
segments and legs than adults, but as they shed
and grow these soon develop.

These tiny 6cm (2in) captive-bred
juvenile Millipedes are ready to
move to a new home and start
their own colony.

Praying Mantis *Sphodromantis sp*

The awesome Praying Mantis is a familiar creature to many people who live in the warmer parts of the world. At least one European type, *Mantis religiosa*, was introduced into the United States early in the last century, and it is now widespread and considered a naturalized species.

Mantids are best held by allowing them to crawl up and on to your hand. They will not tolerate being held between thumb and finger.

Appearance and behaviour

Many varieties are available for the pet keeper, and they are usually green or brown in colour, reaching 7–8cm (3in) in length. One particularly attractive species is the Orchid Mantis (*Hymenopus coronatus*), which is a shade of pink and closely resembles the flower blooms it rests upon whilst awaiting visiting insects. The Praying Mantis is a voracious predator. It can actively stalk its prey or can wait patiently camouflaged against foliage for an insect to venture within striking range. Upon close examination, we can see that Mantids are well designed for killing. The long front legs are lined with numerous spines and a curved hook, which, in a fraction of a second, snatches and impales the unsuspecting insect. Once held, the prey's fate is sealed and the Mantis starts to consume it.

Creating the right environment

Praying Mantids are generally purchased as nymphs, individually packed in small plastic containers. Measuring only a centimetre or so in length, the Mantis needs a twig to climb upon and fruit flies or other mini bugs to feed on. As the Mantis feeds and needs to grow, it will moult, reaching its next development stage, which is known as an instar. After it has moulted several times, larger accommodation should be offered. A 30 x 45 x 30cm (12 x 18 x 12in) vivarium is ideal, and it can be heated, if required, by a spot lamp or heater pad. These creatures like to be kept at a temperature of around 24°C (75°F) - this can drop a few degrees at night with no ill effects.

As arboreal invertebrates, Mantids need to be provided with something to climb upon. Branches, twigs, foliage and other decorations are all suitable and make an attractive home for you and your Mantis to enjoy. A living plant helps to enhance any display. A fluorescent lamp will assist in plant growth as well as light the vivarium to good effect. Mantids are cannibalistic and should be kept individually.

The only insect that can turn its head and look over its 'shoulder' at you, Praying Mantids are a simple to keep pet.

A voracious predator, this Praying Mantis has caught and is consuming a cricket.

Handling

For closer examination, you can encourage a Mantis onto the palm of your hand, where it will move around quite happily. Don't attempt to pick one up using a finger or thumb because the Mantis will jab you with its forearms. Be warned that adult Mantids can fly, so ensure that all the doors and windows are closed just in case.

Feeding

Mantids will eat almost any live foods they can catch and hold on to. The very smallest need fruit flies, micro crickets or aphids, but once they begin to grow they will quickly graduate to larger prey, such as crickets, butterflies and houseflies. In the wild, even bees and wasps will be eaten. Feed them as much as they will eat, but do not leave too much live food in the vivarium as they can distress the Mantis if it feels overrun. They are messy feeders, leaving discarded legs, wings and other body parts lying around the vivarium. These should be removed regularly, along with any mantis faecal pellets.

Breeding

Mantids are essentially an annual species, with offspring emerging each spring. If lucky, they survive to mature, mate and, if female, lay eggs before dying within the same year. Your pet Mantis is therefore relatively short lived, taking six months to mature and then living for approximately six months as an adult. By growing on several nymphs to maturity, you have a good chance of breeding them. Females are easily distinguished from males: they have six visible segments on the underside of their abdomen, whereas males have eight. Mating is a dangerous time for males – they may be eaten attempting to mate, during mating or immediately afterwards. One female may produce several egg cases (oothecae) from a successful mating. Even unmated females will lay eggs, but these won't hatch.

The new generation emerge in great numbers from each egg case, which may contain 20–200 eggs. Newly-emerged Mantids are the size of a mosquito and are miniature versions of the adults. Like all insects, by the time they have reached adulthood they have wings and can fly. The appearance of wings establishes that maturity has been reached and the Mantids are ready to breed.

Known as an oothecae, the numerous baby Mantis eggs are well protected inside the hardened foam egg case.

Hermit Crab *Ceonobita sp.*

Land Hermit Crabs are found in the warmer parts of the world, including America, Australia and Asia. They are well adapted for life on land, burrowing into sand or under tree roots in humid habitats. Depending on where you live, up to 13 species are known and several make interesting pets.

must know

Hermit Crabs return to the sea to breed with the eggs hatching into tiny free-swimming larvae that eventually return to dry land as tiny crabs, so they will not breed in captivity. Fortunately, most species are very common and live longer as pets than in the wild.

Appearance and behaviour

Hermit Crabs are available in a variety of colours, ranging from pink or reddish brown to sandy yellow. They use the empty shells of other marine or land snails as a home and for protection, changing these regularly as they moult and grow. They vary in size quite considerably, from 5cm (2in) up to 15cm (6in), and live for over 10 years.

Creating the right environment

Hermit Crabs are, in fact, very social animals and should be kept in groups. They are active mostly at night. A substrate of either fine beach sand or coral and reef sands is fine, but some people keep them successfully on river pebbles and/or coconut fibre. The important thing is that they need to burrow, especially when a moult is due. The larger the aquarium/vivarium you can provide, the better for offering a range of substrates at varying depths. They need to be heated to between 22–27°C (72–80°F), if you do not have a warm enough house, by heater pads or a lamp – follow the instructions carefully. Humidity of 70–80 per cent, without allowing the air to stagnate, is important.

An absolute necessity is plenty of options for

changing shells. Any pet store that sells these crabs should have a selection of sizes and types to tempt your growing pet into selecting some more suitable accommodation. Some will change shells every few weeks given the opportunity. Children are particularly drawn to the highly coloured painted shells at pet shops, but a variety of options is more important to the crab than colour.

Initially nervous of handling, this Hermit Crab has retreated into its shell for protection.

Handling

These crabs are generally non aggressive but can pinch with their claws. Simply lift them by the shell and place on your hand. As they get accustomed to you, they will amble about quite happily from hand to hand, retreating into the shell when nervous. Make sure you are seated to ensure that you do not drop them, especially if they pinch you with their claws. Never ever try to pull one from its shell.

Much enjoyment can be gained from watching these comical creatures shuffle around the vivarium looking for food and new accommodation.

Feeding

These are omnivorous scavengers, so almost anything goes foodwise. Pet shops frequently sell Hermit Crab foods and these are usually good enough, but they will also eat small pieces of carrot, banana, coconut, fish flakes and pellets, salad leaves and even bits of meat. Avoid citrus fruits and anything spicy or processed. They will benefit from natural unbleached beach debris, such as cuttle fish, driftwood and natural corals and sponges, which will be nibbled at. A shallow bowl of fresh water and another of salty sea water are recommended, along with a shallow food bowl that is changed before spoiling.

Moulting

At regular intervals, Hermit Crabs need to moult. This is the trickiest part of their care to get right. Generally they become sluggish before a moult and may even appear 'dead' if you are not used to this change. They either hide under a root or burrow into a sandy mixture in a damper part of their home. They are most vulnerable at this time and are best removed from a colony to a separate moulting tank until the process is completed. At this stage, some new shell options will be appreciated and they will be very keen to feed. They must be kept humid.

Unlike these rather plain old sea shells, glossy painted shells that are suitable for Hermit Crabs can be bought at many pet stores.

Curly-haired Tarantula
Brachypelma albopilosa

There are around 800 species of Tarantula. These large, hairy spiders often have appealing colours and markings and make a popular low-cost pet, requiring only the minimum of time and space to maintain them in excellent condition.

Popular pets

It is best to buy one as a spiderling and they are bred in large numbers in Europe and America to satisfy demand. The most popular and passive are those from North, Central and South America. One of these, the Curly-haired Tarantula, is a favourite of mine, and I have a specimen of around 30 years of age that has been handled for many years without ever once causing me any concerns.

Creating the right environment

Most Tarantulas not only thrive in but also seem to prefer small vivariums, and although some species may live communally, the Curly-haired and other terrestrial species featured in this book should be housed alone. A 30 x 30 x 30cm (12 x 12 x 12in) vivarium is fine, although a larger unit does give you more scope to create an attractive naturalistic display. They need a retreat and some peat, wood chips or vermiculite mixed together to make a good substrate. Maintain at 24–29°C (75–84°F).

Handling

Not everyone wants to handle their pet Tarantula and that is fine, but should you wish to, then it is

must know

No record can be found of human deaths caused by a Tarantula bite – they are not a species considered dangerous to man. They are usually portrayed as aggressive and deadly, but whilst they are predators and do have large fangs most are very mild mannered and are unlikely to even try to bite their carer.

Despite their fearsome reputation, many Tarantulas make attractive if somewhat unusual pets.

important to never drop your pet. Although these spiders are robust animals, the legs and abdomen can be injured easily in a fall. They should not be allowed to climb onto clothing as the tiny hooks in their legs get stuck in material. Tarantulas can bite, but it is a rare event. However, the abdominal hairs can cause an allergic reaction, so be careful not to touch them here – just stroke the legs.

Feeding

Most pet spiders like mine live on a diet of crickets. Variety is good, however, and occasionally I will offer something different, such as a non-toxic caterpillar, beetle grub or locust hopper. In the wild, they would attempt to eat almost any small vertebrate or invertebrate they can overpower.

Breeding

Breeding Tarantulas provides a fascinating insight into the precarious mating habits of spiders. You are, if successful, likely to feel euphoric at your achievement in helping to bring new lives into the world (400–600 of them). Considerable time and effort will be required to ensure their initial survival and subsequent development. A male that is ready to mate will deposit some sperm onto a small sheet of web. He will then dip his pedipalp into the sperm and proceed to visit any potential mates. The females release an attractant scent that draws him into a potentially fatal meeting. If the male finds a willing partner, he will hold her fangs with his mating hooks and insert and empty his sperm into her genital opening. So far so good – he will then beat a hasty retreat although frequently she will turn on him and eat him.

Moulting spiders

When a Tarantula is found upside down with curled-up legs, it is probably just moulting. Do not disturb it but remove any uneaten live foods still present in the vivarium. It can take between one and two days for an adult to complete the process. Spiderlings moult very regularly because they grow quickly. Adults do so less frequently, moulting on average once a year. Soon after moulting or shedding, Tarantulas are normally keen to drink and feed but it takes another day or so for their new exoskeleton to harden completely.

Always handle your pet with care. Many Tarantula owners regularly handle their spiders but ensure that they do so with caution.

Mexican Red Kneed Tarantula
Brachypelma smithi

These are one of the most striking Tarantulas – large with a leg span of 15–18cm (6–7in). The body is dark brown with bright red on all eight leg joints and pedipalps, making them a popular pet. Females can live for 30 years but a male's life span is more limited.

must know

This spider is a protected and threatened species with its natural habitat along the central Pacific coast in Mexico under continuing pressure from land clearing for ranching, agriculture and housing. However, fortunately for the pet keeper, they are widely bred in captivity.

Creating the right environment

These spiders inhabit dry, scrubby desert but like humidity levels of around 70 per cent. A shallow water dish helps provide this as well as drinking water. A mix of vermiculite and peat or wood chips 9cm (3^1/$_2$in) deep provides ample opportunity to dig a burrow.

A piece of cork bark or half a flower pot on its side can be used as a retreat. A minimum vivarium size of 30 x 30 x 30cm (12 x 12 x 12in) is adequate, warmed from below by a heater pad covering no more than half the area and controlled by a thermostat to 24–28°C (75–82°F).

Alternatively, a lamp over part of the unit may be used to warm the spiders.

Handling

Handling should be initiated at an early age, so the spider and handler gradually get used to each other. The spider should be gently nudged on the legs to encourage it to walk onto your hands. Occasionally skittish, take great care to avoid touching the urticating (stinging/itching) hairs of the abdomen that may be rubbed off in a 'cloud' when the spider is irritated. Always wash your hands after touching Tarantulas and remember that many people keep them but never ever try or want to handle them.

Feeding

This spider is a nocturnal hunter with the tips of all its legs very sensitive to smells, tastes and vibration. It will tackle a variety of prey from insects to frogs, lizards and rodents.

The prey is held and venom is injected from both fangs to paralyse it and begin digestion before the body is sucked dry, leaving a hollow skin or exoskeleton behind. In captivity, crickets are the established offering, but locusts and other prey can be offered for variety.

must know

To breed these spiders, see page 181. Mexican Red Kneed and other Tarantula males can, upon maturing, moult, and they are readily identified by the two mating hooks on the underside of the front pair of legs.

This species is traditionally used for human contact at many zoos and wildlife parks. However, some individuals are easily irritated and would not be suitable for handling.

Chilean Rose Tarantula *Grammostola rosea*

These are attractive, rather fluffy-looking spiders with a salmon pink or rosy red hue. They are often seen on breeders' lists or in pet stores at 2–3cm (1in) in size – the ideal time to acquire one. They occur in South America in Chile, Argentina and Bolivia.

must know

Confusingly for the hobbyist, this species has undergone several taxonomic (science of classification) name changes, and you may see them in books or on websites as *Grammostola cala* or *spatulata* and now *rosea*. However, they are always commonly referred to as Chilean Rose Tarantulas.

Creating the right environment

Chilean Rose Tarantulas should always be kept alone; like most spiders, they are not social animals. They are content and safe on their own and do not feel lonely. This species is less likely to use burrows than many other Tarantula types but must still be offered a retreat or two to hide in. I have kept them in the larger plastic pet homes but a 30 x 30 x 30cm (12 x 12 x 12in) vivarium is just fine. They need to be kept warm at around 26–28°C (79–82°F) but not as warm as some species – a warm room is likely to be sufficient. If you can give one a larger vivarium of,

It is amazing to see how arthropods change their exoskeleton to grow and you have a good chance of observing this with spiders.

say, 60 x 30 x 30cm (24 x 12 x 12in) with multiple retreats and heat the warm part of the unit with a lamp or heat pad, but, judging by where they prefer to live, you will get a good understanding of their preferences. A 5–6cm (2in) depth of vermiculite mix or peat is good as a base, and a couple of retreats should be provided along with a very shallow water dish. Probably once, maybe twice, a year a clean out is required. Move your spider to a small escape-proof tub while you thoroughly clean the entire unit, replacing the old substrate.

Tarantulas can be handled on a regular basis without incident. Their dangerous image belies their usually gentle nature.

Handling

This is another popular handling species, but adult attention should always be given when children are attempting to pick up a spider, and great care taken to avoid the irritating hairs of the abdomen.

Feeding

Most captive-reared Tarantulas live pretty much on crickets, locusts or hoppers. As with all live foods, it is important that they have been well fed and cared for to ensure their nutritious content. A few bugs can be left with the spider, so it can hunt at will, apart from when a moult is due. If the spider seems irritated by excess live food, remove it at once.

Breeding

Female Chilean Rose Tarantulas probably live for around 15 years in captivity whilst males reach a final maturing moult at around two years of age. Their days are then very much numbered.

Imperial Scorpion *Pandinus imperator*

These giant scorpions are the world's largest, up to 20cm (8in), but they are easy to care for and not dangerous. Native to Central and West African forests, they hide beneath rotten logs and leaf litter.

must know

With savage pincers and a poison gland in her tail, an amorous male approaches a female with great caution. He grabs her pincers, and, with her weapons safely controlled, they dance, shuffling forwards and backwards. The male deposits a pack of sperm on the ground and, as he pulls her over it, the female takes up the tiny package into her body. To avoid becoming her supper, the male quickly releases his hold and they separate.

Creating the right environment

Spending time hidden or hunting in leaf litter, the Imperial Scorpion likes a good ground covering. A depth of up to 15cm (6in) of peat/vermiculite and leaf litter will replicate its forest habitat. A retreat is essential to make it feel secure. A small colony of four to ten scorpions may be housed together for breeding purposes, so long as ample retreats and food are available. A vivarium measuring 120 x 30 x 30cm (48 x 12 x 12in) is adequate. Some fighting is inevitable within a colony, and occasionally a specimen may be devoured by its 'friends'. For this reason, many people prefer to keep them separately. Heating by pad is recommended, as they need ground warmth, to 25–30°C (77–86°F). Mist spray regularly to maintain humidity levels, and provide a very shallow water dish.

Handling

Most people keep these scorpions for their aesthetic pleasure and enjoy watching their behaviour. I don't recommend that novices or young people handle scorpions. However, some people do enjoy picking them up by quickly and firmly holding the scorpion by its bulbous sting and placing it in the palm of the hand. However, be warned as temperaments vary. They can pinch very hard with their claws and a sting will hurt, but generally this species is passive.

Feeding

As predatory arachnids, these creatures prefer slow-moving prey, such as large grubs and caterpillars. Dead mice, pinkies, locusts and crickets are all taken. Offer food twice weekly by releasing insects into the vivarium or by offering food, using long tweezers, directly to the scorpion's pincers.

Breeding

After mating (see opposite), eventually some 20–50 live young appear as small white spots crawling on the mother's back. Once the young have moulted and darkened, they leave the mother to fend for themselves. At this stage they should be separated from the parent's vivarium. Maturing Imperial Scorpions shed their exoskeleton about once a year.

These giant African Scorpions, unlike many of their relatives, are not considered dangerous.

want to know more?

• Information about invertebrates can be found in most local libraries and book stores as well as on the internet. Look at the following websites:
www.si.edu
www.bugwise.net.au
www.whatsthatbug.com

Need to know more?

Clubs and societies

Amateur Entomological Society (AES)
PO Box 8774
London
SW7 5ZG
www.ex.ac.uk/bugclub

Association for the Study of Reptiles and Amphibians
PO Box 73
Banbury
Oxon
OX15 8RE
www.amentsoc.org

British Herpetological Society
c/o Zoological Society of London
Regent's Park
London
NW1 4RY
www.bhs.org

International Herpetological Society
22 Busheyfields Road
Russsells Hall
Dudley
West Midlands
DY1 2LP
www.international-herpetological-society.org

British Chelonia Group
Society promoting the care of tortoises and turtles.
www.britishcheloniagroup.org.uk

Federation of British Herpetologists
This exists to promote and support the responsible breeding of reptiles and amphibians by individuals in the UK.
www.f-b-h.co.uk

Websites and magazines

There are numerous websites and magazines that are dedicated to the care of reptiles, amphibians and invertebrates. They are also a good source of up-to-date information on events and shows. Using the internet, you can find information that is relevant to you and where you live. Listed below are some useful resources.

British Tarantula Society (BTS)
www.thebts.co.uk

Reptiles Magazine
A monthly American published magazine also available in Europe with a good website.
www.reptilesmagazine.com

Reptile Hobbyist Magazine
An American publication.
www.tfh.com

Reptilia Magazine
A European bi-monthly magazine,
published in Spanish, German, English
and Italian editions.
www.reptilia.net

Kingsnake.com
A web portal for all herpetologists,
this will help you find internet links to
breeders and dealers as well as general
information on reptiles from sites all
over the world.
www.kingsnake.com

Further reading

Arnold, E.N., and Burton, J.A., *A Field
Guide to the Reptiles and Amphibians of
Britain and Europe* (HarperCollins, 1996)
Bateman, Rev. Gregory, *The Vivarium*
(Upcott Gill, 1897)
Bellairs, A., and Carrington, R., *The World
of Reptiles* (Chatto and Windus, 1966)
Berenbaum, May R., *Bugs in the System*
(Addison Wesley, 1995)
Fabre, J.H., *The Insect World of J. Henri
Fabre* (Beacon Press, Boston, 1991)
Ferguson, G., and de Vosjoli, P. (Eds.),
*Care and Breeding Panther, Veiled and
Parsons Chameleons* (Advanced Vivarium
Systems, USA, 1995)
Mattison, Chris, *Care of Reptiles &
Amphibians in Captivity* (Blandford
Press, 1983)
Mehrtens, John M., *Living Snakes of the
World* (Sterling Publishing Co, 1987)
Necas, Petr, *Chameleons: Nature's Hidden
Jewels* (Krieger Publishing, 1999)
Pfeffer, Pierre (Ed.), *Predators and
Predation* (Facts on File Inc., New
York, 1989)
Smith, Hobart M., *Handbook of Lizards*
(Comstock Publishing, 1946)
de Vosjoli, Phillipe, *General Care
and Maintenance of Leopard Geckos*
(Advanced Vivarium Systems, USA, 1990)
de Vosjoli, Phillipe, *Lizard Keeper's
Handbook* (Advanced Vivarium Systems,
USA, 1994)

Acknowledgements

Thanks to Jenny, Jack and Georgia,
Simon Murrell, Jed Currey, and all the
snakes, lizards and invertebrates that
know me.

Index

abscesses 37
African Clawed Frog 54–55
American Green Toad 58–59
American Green Tree Frog 66–67
amphibians 7, 16, 39, 40–69
Argentinean Horned Frog 62–63
arthropods 165
Australian Green Tree Frog 64–65
Axolotl 44–47
bacterial infections 39
Bearded Dragon 20, 29, 90–93
blisters 38
Black Headed Python 146–147
Blue-tongued Skink 29, 86–89
Boa Constrictor 158–161
Brazilian Rainbow Boa 156–157
Bull Snake 154–155
Californian Kingsnake 120–123
captive breeding 8, 42
carnivores 32–33, 164
Carpet Python 148–149
chameleons 6, 94–99
   Panther Chameleon 96–99
   Veiled Chameleon 20, 29, 94–95
Children's Python 144–145
Chilean Rose Tarantula 184–185
conservation 7
choosing pets 12–17
Common Garter Snake 38, 150–151
Corn Snake 128–131
Couch's Spadefoot Toad 60–61
crustaceans 165
Curly-haired Tarantula 179–181
dehydration 37
ectotherms 164
equipment 21–25
feeding 28–35, 164

Fire Salamander 52–53
frogs 6, 42, 43
   African Clawed Frog 54–55
   American Green Tree Frog 66–67
   Argentinean Horned Frog 62–63
   Australian Green Tree Frog 64–65
   Green Tree Frog 8
   Red-eyed Tree Frog 68–69
full spectrum lighting 21, 22, 37
geckos 16, 20
   Giant Day Gecko 82–83
   Leopard Gecko 9, 36, 74–77
   Peacock Day Gecko 78–79
   Standing's Day Gecko 80–81
Giant Day Gecko 82–83
Giant Millipede 170–171
Green Anole 29, 84–85
Green Iguana 108–111
Green Tree Frog 8
handling pets 15–17, 164–165
health 36–39
heaters 22
herbivores 28–29, 164
Hermit Crab 165, 176–178
hides 23
House Snake 134–135
housing pets 18–27
iguanas 6
   Green Iguana 108–111
Imperial Scorpion 186–187
Indian Stick Insect 166–167
insectivores 30–31
invertebrates 17, 162–187
Kingsnakes 33
   Californian Kingsnake 120–123
Latin names 14–15
Leaf Insect 164, 168–169

Leopard Gecko 9, 36, 74–77
lizards 16, 28, 29, 37, 38, 72–111
  sexing 93
Metabolic Bone Disease 21, 37
Mexican Red Kneed Tarantula 182–183
millipedes 165, 170–171
mist spraying 37
mites 38, 165
obesity 36
Oriental Fire-bellied Toad 56–57
Paddle-tailed Newt 50–51
Panther Chameleon 96–99
parasites 38
Peacock Day Gecko 78–79
plants 24–25
Plumed Basilisk 106–107
Praying Mantis 35, 164, 172–175
python(s) 7
  Black Headed Python 146–147
  Carpet Python 148–149
  Children's Python 144–145
  Royal Python 7, 33, 136–139
  Sand Python 140–143
rearing containers 13
Red-eyed Tree Frog 68–69
Red-spotted Newt 48–49
reptiles 70–161
Rough Green Snake 152–153
Royal Python 7, 33, 136–139
salmonellosis 39
Sand Python 140–143
Savannah Monitor 102–103
scales 119
scorpions 165, 186–187
Sinloan Milk Snake 124–127
sloughing 35, 38, 42
snakes 16–17, 32–33, 37, 38, 118–161
  Black Headed Python 146–147
  Boa Constrictor 158–161
  Brazilian Rainbow Boa 156–157
  Bull Snake 154–155

Californian Kingsnake 120–123
Carpet Python 148–149
Children's Python 144–145
Common Garter Snake 38, 150–151
Corn Snake 128–131
House Snake 134–135
Rough Green Snake 152–153
Royal Python 7, 33, 136–139
Sand Python 140–143
Sinloan Milk Snake 124–127
Woma 140–143
Yellow Rat Snake 132–133
spiders 164, 165
  Chilean Rose Tarantula 184–185
  Curly-haired Tarantula 179–181
  Mexican Red Kneed Tarantula 182–183
spotlights 22
Spur-thighed Tortoise 112–115
Standing's Day Gecko 80–81
stick insects 164, 166–167
substrates 25–27, 39
thermometers 21
thermoregulation 20
thermostats 22
toads 20
  American Green Toad 58–59
  Couch's Spadefoot Toad 60–61
  Oriental Fire-bellied Toad 56–57
tortoises 28, 72–73, 112–115
  Spur-thighed Tortoise 112–115
Uromastyx 100–101
Veiled Chameleon 20, 29, 94–95
vivariums 10–39
  glass 18
  lighting and heating 19–22
  plastic 19
  wood 19
water 23, 37, 39
Water Dragon 104–105
Woma 140–143
Yellow Rat Snake 132–133

⚙ Collins need to know?

**Look out for these recent titles in Collins' practical and accessible
need to know? series.**

Other titles in the series:

Antique Marks
Aquarium Fish
Birdwatching
Body Language
Buying Property in France
Buying Property in Spain
Calorie Counting
Card Games
Card Making
Chess
Children's Parties
Codes & Ciphers
Decorating
Detox
Digital Photography
DIY
Dog and Puppy Care

Dog Training
Downloading
Drawing & Sketching
Dreams
Fertility & Conception
First Aid
Food Allergies
Golf
Guitar
Horse and Pony Care
How to Lose Weight
Kama Sutra
Kings and Queens
Knots
Low GI/GL Diet
Mushroom Hunting
NLP

Outdoor Survival
Party Games
Pilates
Poker
Pregnancy
Property
Sleep
Speak French
Speak Italian
Speak Spanish
Stargazing
Watercolour
Weather Watching
Weddings
Wine
Woodworking
The World

Universe
Yoga
Zodiac Types

**To order any of these
titles, please telephone
0870 787 1732 quoting
reference 263H.
For further information
about all Collins books,
visit our website:
www.collins.co.uk**